JN105445

増補改訂版

災害時の英語

デイビッド・A・セイン

Preface

In light of the 2020 Corona-virus outbreak, this book has been updated to include additional phrases and information for infectious diseases. I hope that this will further help in ensuring the health and safety of all those affected by such disasters.

Although disasters, accidents and terrorism ar things that no one wishes to be involved in during the lifetime, it's not unimaginable to think that you could b caught up in one today. This book has been written t enable you to be of assistance in protecting the live of the foreigners and English speakers around you times of an unexpected calamity.

There are a large number of phrases for communicatir with English-speaking people during disaster including earthquakes and other disasters set off b earthquakes, such as tsunamis, fires and nuclea accidents. Expressions used for other calamities lik typhoons and snow damage, life in evacuation cente and everyday preparations are included as well.

This book contains phrases usable right off th bat for making quick in-building announcements giving evacuation instructions, making it an invaluab reference for staff to keep on hand at hotels, store and public facilities.

I hope to encourage Japanese to inform and offer helping hand to non-Japanese speakers around yo during an eventful situation or disaster. It is my deepe wish that this book proves helpful for that purpose.

David A. Thay

この<増補改訂版>では、2020年の新型コロナウイルスの流行を受けて、感染症に関するフレーズや情報を追加しました。災害に遭われた方々の健康と安全の確保に、本書がより一層のお役に立つことを願っております。

「災害」や「事故」、「テロ」といった出来事には、だれもが関わることなく一生を終えられたらと願うものですが、残念ながらだれもが今日巻き込まれてもおかしくありません。本書は、そんな予期せず降りかかる災難から、あなたの周りにいる外国人の「いのちを守る」ために役立ててほしいという思いでつくられました。

「津波」や「火事」、「原発事故」といった二次災害を引き起こす恐れのある「地震」を中心に、「台風」や「雪害」といった「その他の災害」や「避難所生活」、そして「日頃の備え」まで、英語話者とのコミュニケーションに使えるフレーズを多数収載しています。

さらに、施設などのスタッフとして、館内アナウンスや避難誘導の必要に迫られた場合にそのまま使える表現も盛り込まれているので、ホテルや店舗、公共施設に常備していただきたい1冊に仕上がっています。

「災害」という「非日常」においても周りの非日本語話者を意識し、手を差し伸べる気持ちを持っていただけたら幸いです。本書がその際の一助となるよう心から願っています。

デイビッド・A・セイン

本書の構成および利用法

本書は災害の状況別に「重要フレーズ」を紹介しています。また、効率的に情報を伝達するための「標識・ポスター」見本も掲載しています。

災害がいつ起こるかは、誰にもわかりません。日頃の防災の一助として、本書に普段から目を通し、「いざ」というときに備えましょう。非常用持ち出し袋の中など、非常時にすぐ取り出せる場所に入れておくこともお薦めします。

重要フレーズ

周囲の外国人の安全を確保するために、これだけは伝えられるようになりたい。そんな重要フレーズを災害の規模別、状況別に紹介しています。

標識・ポスター

注意事項を文字にして掲示すると、効率的に情報を伝達できます。緊急時や災害時に必要となる標識やポスターの見本も紹介しています。

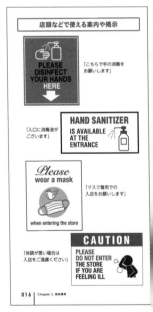

音声のダウンロード方法

本書掲載の「重要フレーズ」の音声を無料でダウンロードしていただけます。

アスク出版ウェブサイトからのダウンロード

弊社ウェブサイトから、パソコンやスマートフォンにダウンロードできます。

① ウェブブラウザを使って、以下のサイトにアクセス

https://www.ask-books.com/

② 検索フォームから「災害時の英語」と検索

③ 「詳細を見る」をクリック

検索結果に本書が表示されます。詳細ページに進むと、「音声ダウンロード」という項目があるので、そこからダウンロード可能です（※）。

音声ファイルは、本書のページごとに分割されており、ページ番号がファイル名になっています。

※ダウンロード後、お使いの音声再生アプリ（iTunes など）に取り込む方法については、各メーカーにお問い合わせください。

audiobook.jp からダウンロード

株式会社オトバンクが提供するオーディオブック配信サービスからダウンロードすることも可能です。まず audiobook.jp に会員登録（無料）していただき、ご利用ください。

利用方法については、以下のサイトをご覧ください。

https://audiobook.jp/exchange/ask-books

シリアルコード

audiobook.jp からダウンロードする場合には、下記シリアルコードの入力が必要です。

93582

CONTENTS

Chapter 2　小〜中規模の災害

Chapter 3　大規模災害

hapter 5　その他の災害および事故・事件

Chapter 6　防災意識を高める

ppendix　災害時に役立つ資料集

Chapter 1

感染爆発

店頭などで使える案内や掲示

「こちらで手の消毒を
お願いします」

「入口に消毒液が
ございます」

「マスク着用での
入店をお願いします」

「体調が悪い場合は
入店をご遠慮ください」

※以下の案内と掲示の PDF データを弊社ウェブサイトからダウンロードできます。5 ページの音声ダウンロードと同じ方法で、本書紹介ページにアクセスしてください。

「レジでは、お互いに
2メートル離れて
お並びください」

「お持ち帰りできます」

「こちらでお待ちください」

「マスクはおひとり様
1袋まで」

1. Wet your hands with water.
手を水で濡らす

2. Apply soap.
石けんをつける

3. Rub the palms of your hands together
手のひらをこすり合わせる

4. Rub the backs of your hands while interlacing your fingers.
両手の指を交差させながら手の甲をこする

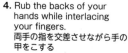
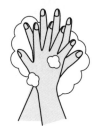

5. Rub palms together while interlacing your fingers.
両手の指を交差させながら手のひらを合わせてこする

6. Wrap your fingers with backs of fingers to opposing palms.
両手の指を組んで、指の背を反対の手のひらに押し付けてこする

7. Clasp your thumbs in your opposite hand and rub.
親指を反対の手で強く握り、こする

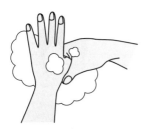

10. Rinse your hands with water.
水で手を洗い流す

8. Rub the tips of your fingers in the palm of the opposing hand.
指の先を反対の手のひらにこすりつけて洗う

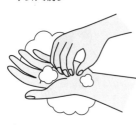

11. Thoroughly dry your hands.
手を完全に乾かす

9. Rub your wrists with the opposite hand.
手首を反対の手で洗う

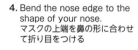

1. Clean your hands with soap and water or hand sanitizer.
   石けんと水、もしくは手指消毒剤で手をきれいにする

4. Bend the nose edge to the shape of your nose.
   マスクの上端を鼻の形に合わせて折り目をつける

2. Avoid touching the front side of the mask.
   マスクのおもて面には触らない

5. Pull the bottom of the mask over your mouth and chin.
   口とあごを覆うようにマスクの下端をひっぱる

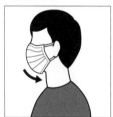

3. Hold the mask by the ear loops, and place them around your ears (with the colored side of the mask, if there is one, facing out).
   耳にかけるひもの部分でマスクを持ち、耳にひもをかける（マスクに色の付いた面があるならば、その面を外側に）

1. Avoid touching the front
side of the mask.
マスクのおもて面には触らない

3. Dispose of the mask.
マスクを捨てる

2. Hold the mask by the ear
loops, and remove them
from your ears.
耳ひも部分を持ち、耳からひも
を外す

4. Clean your hands with
soap and water or hand
sanitizer.
石けんと水、もしくは手指消毒
剤で手をきれいにする

▶ 簡単手作りマスクの作り方 How to make a simple homemade mask

What you need（必要な物）:

● handkerchief, bandana or other similarly sized piece of cloth
ハンカチ、バンダナ、もしくは同等サイズの布
● rubber bands or hair ties
輪ゴム、もしくは髪ゴム

1. Lay the cloth flat and fold it in half.
布を平らに広げ、半分に折る

2. Fold the cloth into half or thirds again into a size that fits over your nose and mouth.
自分の鼻と口のサイズに合うよう、さらに半分もしくは3等分に折る

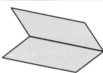

3. Place the rubber bands or hair ties over the fabric about 15 centimeters apart.
輪ゴム・髪ゴムを折った布に通して15 cmほど離して置く

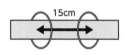

4. Fold the sides in over the middle section.
横側を中央に向けて折る

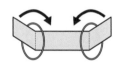

5. Pull the rubber bands or hair ties over your ears.
輪ゴム・髪ゴムを引っ張って耳にかける

風土病	endemic
伝染病、伝染病の流行	epidemic
伝染病の世界的大流行、感染爆発	pandemic
最初の感染者、感染第一号	patient zero
発生、勃発	outbreak
感染集団	outbreak cluster
感染	infection
汚染	contamination
制御、封じ込め	containment
…の拡散を封じ込める	contain the spread of ...
コロナウイルス	coronavirus
新型コロナウイルス感染症	COVID-19
インフルエンザ	influenza
鳥インフルエンザ	bird flu
豚インフルエンザ	swine flu
空気感染	airborne infection
経口感染	oral infection
飛沫	droplet
マスク	mask, face mask
米国労働安全衛生研究所規格に合格した、医療用の高性能マスク	N-95 mask
フェイスシールド	face shield
(抗菌) 石けん	(antibacterial) soap
殺菌剤	disinfectant
手指消毒剤	hand sanitizer
除菌用ウェットティッシュ	antibacterial wet wipes
空気清浄機	air purifier
換気扇	ventilator
買いだめ	hoarding
検査	testing
PCR 検査	PCR test
抗体検査	antibody test
(病気) にかかる	contract
症状、徴候	symptom
自覚症状のない	asymptomatic
濃厚接触者	close contact

免疫系	immune system
ワクチン	vaccine
死亡率	mortality rate
緊急事態(を宣言する/解除する)	(declare / lift) state of emergency
3密	Three Cs (closed spaces, crowded places, close-contact settings)
封鎖、ロックダウン	lockdown
(伝染病予防のための) 隔離	quarantine
自主隔離	self-quarantine
入国制限	immigration restriction
移動禁止、渡航禁止	travel ban
移動制限、渡航制限	travel restriction
社会的距離をとること	social distancing
じっとしていて気が変になる	go stir crazy
リモートで働く	work remotely
(グラフの曲線を平らにする) 上昇率を抑える	flatten the curve

感染経路について

このウイルスの感染者全員が発症するわけではありません	Not all people who contract the virus show symptoms.
新型コロナウイルスの潜伏期間は1日から14日です	The incubation period of COVID-19 ranges from 1 to 14 days.
症状がいちばん重いときに、最も人にうつしやすいとされています	People are thought to be most contagious when they are most symptomatic.
このウイルスは飛沫によって近距離を移動し、口や鼻から体内に取り込まれます	The virus can be carried within droplets over a short distance and can be inhaled through the mouth or nose.
ペットがこのウイルスを拡散させている事例は、少ないです	There have been a small number of cases of pets spreading the virus.
このウイルスは屋外では拡散しにくいそうです	I read that the virus doesn't spread as easily outdoors.
混雑していないかぎり、プールで感染する可能性は高くありません	Your chances of contracting it in a pool aren't too high as long as there aren't too many people.
無症状のウイルス保持者も、他人に感染させる可能性があります	People who are asymptomatic but carry the virus can still spread it to others.

このウイルスは物の表面を介しても感染しますが、主な感染経路は人対人の接触です	The virus can be transmitted on surfaces, but most infections come from person-to-person contact.
小包や買い物袋など、物の表面を伝って感染するリスクは、比較的低いです	The risk of transmission from packages, grocery bags and other surfaces is relatively low.
新型コロナウイルスが空気で運ばれるという証拠があります	There is evidence that the novel coronavirus may in fact be airborne.
新型コロナウイルスについて、非常に多くのことが不明のままです	So much about COVID-19 remains unknown.
このウイルスは季節性で、夏には消滅すると予測する専門家もいました	Some experts speculated that the virus could be seasonal and may possibly go away in the summer.

▶ 症状について

新型ウイルスの症状は、熱、咳、息切れです。	The symptoms of the new virus include fever, cough and shortness of breath.
新型コロナウイルス感染患者の約15％が入院を要します	Roughly 15 percent of COVID-19 patients may require hospitalization.
新型コロナウイルス感染者の多くは、軽いインフルエンザのような症状ですみます	Most people infected with COVID-19 experience only mild flu-like symptoms.

深刻な肺炎や卒中、神経疾患を引き起こす人もいます	Some can develop severe pneumonia, stroke or neurological diseases.
専門家の試算によると、新型コロナウイルス感染者の35〜50%は無症状です	Experts estimate that 35 to 50 percent of COVID-19 infections are symptomless.
年配者と慢性疾患のある人は、感染リスクが高いでしょう	The risk of infection may be higher for the elderly and people with chronic medical conditions.
このウイルスに感染することで、再感染を防げるかどうかは不明です	We don't know whether having the virus will protect you from catching it again.
このウイルスに感染しても抗体ができるとはかぎりません	Having the virus does not guarantee that you will develop antibodies.
このウイルスに対するワクチンはまだ開発中です	A vaccine for the virus has not yet been developed.

予防法・治療法を説明する

▶予防法について

最低20秒間、手を洗ってください	Make sure to wash your hands for at least 20 seconds.
ドアの所にある手指消毒剤で除菌してください	You can use the hand sanitizer by the door to disinfect your hands.
人が密集した場所や換気が不十分な場所は避けましょう	Avoid crowded areas and poorly ventilated spaces.
マスク着用は、ウイルスの拡散防止に高い効果があると証明されています	Wearing facemasks has been proven to be highly effective in preventing the spread of viruses
感染防止のために、手洗い時に毎回うがいするとよいですよ	It's a good idea to gargle every time you wash your hands to prevent infection.
感染していないことを確認するため、毎朝、検温しましょう	Try to check your temperature every morning to make sure you're not infected.
部屋の換気をよくするために窓を開けましょう	Let's open some windows to keep the room well-ventilated.
咳やくしゃみをするときは、ティッシュや肘の内側で口を覆ってください	Please cover your mouth with a tissue or your elbow when you cough or sneeze.

コを手で覆うの
は、手に病原菌を
広げるだけです

Covering your mouth with your hand will only spread germs to your hands.

感染につながる恐
れがあるので、手
で顔を触らないよ
うに

Try not to touch your face, as doing so could lead to infection.

接触確認アプリを
利用してください

Be sure to use contact tracing apps.

ビタミンCの十分
な摂取は、免疫を
強くし、重度の感
染症の予防に役立
ちます

Getting plenty of vitamin C can help strengthen your immune system and protect against severe infection.

くと石けんがない
場合は、アルコー
ル製の手指消毒剤
で手を洗浄してく
ださい

Use alcohol-based hand sanitizer to clean your hands when soap and water are not available.

医師によると、衛
生状態を良くし、
顔を覆い、集団交
流を限定すること
が、感染を防ぐ最
善策だそうです

Doctors say the best way to avoid infection is through good hygiene, face coverings and limited group interaction.

ぴったりフィット
して、ろ過能力の
高いマスクが、空
気感染予防には最
適です

High-filtration masks that fit snugly are best for preventing infection from airborne diseases.

クチンができるま
で、このウイル
スを制御するのに
予防がきわめて重
要です

Taking health precautions is vital to controlling the virus until there's a vaccine.

▶感染の疑いのある人に対して

気分が悪ければ、すぐに診察を受けてください	If you feel sick, please get checked out as soon as possible
このウイルスの症状 は、37度5分の熱、倦怠感、息苦しさです ☑ 摂氏（Celsius）ではなく、華氏だと 99.5 degrees Fahrenheit	The symptoms of the virus are a fever of 37.5 degrees Celsius, fatigue and difficulty breathing.
症状が4日間続いたら、地域の保健所に電話してください	If you have symptoms of the virus for four days, call your local public health center.
年配者や免疫不全疾患の方は、これらの症状が2日続いたら、保健所に連絡してください	Elderly people or people who are immunosuppressed should contact a public health center after two days of having those symptoms.
軽症者は、自宅待機を求められています	People with mild symptoms are being asked to stay home.
私は今、3週間の自主隔離中です	I've been in self-quarantine for three weeks now.
友人の夫は、職場で感染しました	My friend's husband contracted the virus at work.
この通りの先にある病院は、多言語サービスをやっていますよ	The hospital down the street offers multilingual support.

▶診察

| 体温を計ります。おでこを見せてください | I'm going to take your temperature. Please show me your forehead. |

怠感や息切れを感じていますか	Have you been experiencing any fatigue or shortness of breath?
食事のとき、ちゃんと味はしますか	Are you able to properly taste food when eating?
嗅覚に異常はありますか	Do you have any problems with your sense of smell?
発熱は何日続いていますか	For how many days have you had a fever?
既往症はありますか	Do you have any preexisting conditions?
では、CTスキャンと血液検査を行いますね	Now, we're going to do a CT scan and blood tests.
現在、新型コロナウイルスに特効がある抗ウイルス治療法はありません	Currently, there is no specific antiviral treatment for COVID-19.

検査

PCR検査を受けるには予約が必要です	You need a reservation in order to receive a PCR test.
新大久保病院でPCR検査を受けられますよ	You can receive PCR tests at Shin-Ohkubo Hospital.
綿棒拭き取り検査を行いますね	I'm going to do a swab test.
この綿棒を鼻に入れます	I'm going to insert this swab into your nose.
頭を後ろにそらして、動かないでください	Please lean your head back and try not to move.

結果がでるまでに3日かかります。	It will take three days before we get the results.
陽性となったら、2週間、家から出られませんよ	If you test positive for the virus, you won't be able to leave your house for two weeks.
この1週間で、あなたが接触した全員を書いてください	Please write down everyone you have been in contact with over the past week.
検査のために医療施設を訪れることは、実は感染リスクを高めることになりえます	Visiting medical institutions to get tested for infection could actually increase your risk of infection.
感染しても、ウイルス数が検知できる最低限度に満たない場合、陰性になることがあります	Even if a person is infected, they could test negative due to not yet having enough virus particle to meet the minimum limit of detection.
WHOは、感染が疑われるケースをすべて検査するよう推奨しています	The World Health Organization suggests testing every suspected case of the virus.

情報を発信する

感染状況について

東京都は昨日、22人の新規感染を確認しました	Tokyo confirmed 22 new cases of the virus yesterday.
この1週間、1日の新規感染者数は50人以下です	There have been less than 50 new cases a day for the past week.
1日当たりの感染者数がついに減少し始めました	The number of daily cases is finally starting to decrease.
最近、若者の感染者数が急増しています	Recently, there has been an uptick in the number of young people getting infected.
感染第1号は、3月末にデンマークへ旅行した男性とされています	It is believed that patient zero was a man traveling to Denmark in late March.
あの病院でクラスターが発生しました	There was a cluster at that hospital.
夜の繁華街で新規感染が連鎖しています	There has been a string of new cases in night-time entertainment districts.
最近の感染者数増加の一因は、ソーシャルディスタンス疲れにあると思います	I think social distancing fatigue is partly to blame for the recent rise in cases of infection.

この国がまだ感染第一波の最中であることに、科学者はおおむね意見が一致しています	Scientists generally agree the country is still in its first wave of infections.
近いうちに感染第二波が来る可能性があります	There could be a second wave of infections coming in the near future.
厚生労働省のウェブサイトに英語情報がありますよ	English information is available on the Ministry of Health, Labour and Welfare's Website.

▶必需品について

まだマスクの在庫がある薬局が近くにありますよ	There is a pharmacy nearby that still has some masks in stock.
政府は全世帯にマスクを配布しました	The government has distributed masks to all households.
これらのマスクは布製で、洗濯可、再利用可です	These masks are made of cloth and are washable and reusable.
近所の店はどこもトイレットペーパーが品切れです	All of the stores in my area are completely out of toilet paper.
ゴム手袋がご入り用ですか	Would you like some plastic gloves?

▶緊急事態宣言の発令

これ以上の経済的損失を抑えるために、政府は緊急事態宣言を発令しました	The government has declared a state of emergency to prevent further economic damage.
不要の外出は避けてください	Please try not to leave your residence any more than you need to.
政府は飲食店に休業要請を出しました	The government has issued a closure request for restaurants.
新型コロナの感染拡大により、主要都市のほとんどは封鎖されています	Following the COVID-19 outbreak, most major cities have been put on lockdown.
感染爆発により、大相撲夏場所は2週間延期されました	The Summer Grand Sumo Tournament has been postponed by two weeks due to the pandemic.

ステイホーム

現在、ステイホームの指示がでています	There is a stay-at-home order in place now.
外出できない場合、健康を維持する方法を見つけてください	If you are stuck at home, it's important to find ways to stay fit and active.
ロックダウン中、パン作りを勉強するといいですよ	During the lockdown, one thing to do might be teaching yourself how to bake bread.

感染爆発

ステイホーム期間中、健康を維持するためにオンラインのヨガグループに参加するといいですよ	You could join an online yoga group to help you stay fit during the stay-at-home order.
ステイホーム期間中、家庭内で問題があれば、誰かに知らせてください	If you're having domestic issues during the stay-at-home order, please let someone know.
毎日、ジャンピングジャック、腕立て、腹筋、スクワット各30回を3セットやりましょう	Try to do three sets of 30 jumping jacks, push-ups, sit-ups and squats every day.

▶入国・出国制限について

その病気の拡散防止のため、渡航禁止令がだされました	A travel ban was put in place to help prevent the spread of the disease.
海外からの入国者は14日間隔離されます	People visiting from overseas must quarantine for 14 days.
日本から出国すると、再入国は認められないでしょう	People leaving Japan will be unable to reenter the country.
最近、海外旅行をした人には移動制限が課されます	Travel restrictions have been imposed for anyone that has recently traveled overseas.
海外からの入国者全員を検査する検査センターが、空港の外に設置されています	Testing centers have been installed outside of the airport to test anyone coming into the country from overseas.

政治・経済への影響

▶政府の対策について

政府は、景気刺激のための現金給付を全住民に行います	The government will be handing out stimulus checks to all residents.
病院の負担軽減のため、政府は患者の受け入れを、ホテルに要請しています	The government has asked several hotels to provide housing for patients to ease the burden on hospitals.
政府の感染爆発対策は不十分だと多くの人が感じています	Many people feel that the government isn't doing enough to deal with the pandemic.

▶経済への影響について

感染爆発の影響で、残念ながら閉店いたします	We're afraid our store is closed due to the effects of the pandemic.
多くのレストランがテイクアウトのサービスを拡大し始めています	Many restaurants have started offering more take-out options.
この地域では、一時休業（シャットダウン）の影響で、複数のレストランが廃業しました	Several restaurants in this area have gone out of business due to shutdowns.
この感染爆発は、観光業に壊滅的な影響をおよぼしています	The pandemic has had a devastating effect on the tourism industry.

感染爆発による一時休業措置の結果、大量の解雇が発生しています

There have been a lot of layoffs due to the pandemic-related shutdowns.

世界的大流行に伴う供給不足は、売上の鈍化を招くでしょう

Pandemic-related supply constraints are expected to slow sales.

膨大な死亡者数に加え、この世界的大流行は多くの国の経済に影響を及ぼしています

In addition to the large number of fatalities, the pandemic has also affected many countries' economies.

自粛解除

活動再開

お店や各種サービスが徐々に再開し始めています	They are gradually going to start reopening stores and services.
市はついに、娯楽施設に対する制限を解除する予定です	The city is finally planning to remove restrictions on entertainment venues.
4カ月の閉鎖を経て、地元の動物園がようやく再開しました	The local zoo has finally reopened after being shut down for four months.
感染爆発はまだ収束していないことを忘れず、用心深くなければいけません	We must remain vigilant and remember that this pandemic is not yet over.

ソーシャルディスタンス

外出時は常にマスクを着けてください	Be sure to wear a mask at all times when going out.
握手を避けて、手を振る、お辞儀をするなどしましょう	Avoid shaking hands with other people and instead try waving or bowing.
ほかの人とは少なくとも2メートル離れてください	Try to stay at least two meters away from other people.
店の入口に利用可能な手指消毒剤があります	There is hand sanitizer available at the entrance of the store.
入店するのにマスク着用を求める店もあります	Some stores may require you to wear a mask to go inside.

マスク未着用のお客さまの入店はお断りしています	I'm afraid we do not allow customers into the store without masks on.
このお店は、同時に入店できる人数を制限しています。	This store only allows a certain number of people in at a time.
マスク着用は面倒ですが、やらなくてはいけません	Wearing a face mask can be a hassle, but it's something that we have to do.
あのレストランは入店できませんが、テイクアウトを行っています	That restaurant has closed its tables to customers but still offers take-out.
大規模集会を避けるため、多くのスポーツイベントや音楽フェスが中止になっています	Many sporting events and music festivals have been canceled to prevent people from gathering in large crowds.

▶テレワーク

週2日はテレワークをしてください	Please work from home twice a week.
Zoomで打ち合わせをしましょう	Let's have a meeting on Zoom.
専門家は、人々に可能なかぎりテレワークするよう求めています	Authorities are asking people to telework as much as possible.
感染拡大を避けるため、多くの会社員がリモートワークを推奨されています	Many employees are being encouraged to work remotely to avoid spreading infection.

学校における対策

当校は臨時休校中です	This school is temporarily closed.
学校閉鎖中、オンライン授業を行います	While schools are temporarily closed, online classes will be held.
毎朝、体温を計り、その結果を記録してください	Please take your temperature and record your results every morning.
全児童、マスク着用での登校をお願いします	All children are required to wear masks to school.
新型コロナウィルスによる閉鎖で、私の学校の入学式は中止になりました	Due to the COVID-19 related shutdowns, our school's entrance ceremony was canceled.
閉鎖期間中、子供たちへの自宅教育に挑戦しましたが、たいへんでした	We tried homeschooling our children during the shutdown, but it was a lot of work.
ソーシャルディスタンスを保ちながら遊べる場所を子供たちに提供することが重要です	It's important to give children a place to play while still maintaining social distance.
今、保育所を見つけるのはとても難しいですよ	It's very difficult to find childcare right now.
多くの保育所が新規申込を受け付けていません	Many daycare centers have stopped accepting new applications.

Chapter 2

小～中規模の災害

揺れを感じたら

▶ 地震に対する反応

地震だ！	It's an earthquake!
もしかして、地震？	Wait... is this an earthquake?
けっこう長く揺れるね	It's kind of long, huh?
まだ揺れてるね	It's still shaking.
震度3くらいかな	It's about a 3 on the JMA intensity scale. ☑ JMA intensity scale は日本の気象庁震度階級示しています。
（揺れが）それほど大きくないね	It's not very big.
また地震だ。最近多いね	Again? They happen frequently these days.

▶ 緊急地震速報を確認する

（携帯・スマホの）緊急地震速報だ	It's my phone's earthquake alarm
館内放送を聞こう	Let's listen to the announcement
テレビをつけて	Turn on the TV.
ラジオを聞いてみよう	Let's listen to the radio.
ネットの地震情報をチェックしよう	Let's check the earthquake information online.

注意を喚起する

頭上に気をつけて	Watch your head.
建物のそばから離れて	Keep away from the sides of buildings.
冷蔵庫が倒れてくるかもしれないから気をつけて	The fridge may fall. Please be careful!
走って逃げると危ないよ	It's dangerous to run when trying to escape.
道路に飛び出さないで	Don't run into the streets.
次のため避難する準備をしておこう	Let's prepare to evacuate just in case.

落ち着かせる

落ち着いてください	Please calm down.
きっとすぐにおさまるよ	It's sure to be over soon.
このくらいの揺れならこの建物は大丈夫だ	This building can handle this kind of shaking.
私がついてるから大丈夫	It's okay. I'm here.
揺れがおさまるまでじっとしていたほうがいいよ	It's best to stay put until the shaking is over.

地震に対応する（屋内）

▶ 具体的な行動を指示する

念のため机の下に潜ってください	Just to be safe, get under your desk.
揺れがおさまるまでその場を動かないで	Please stay there until the shaking stops.
窓から離れたところに待機しましょう	Let's wait somewhere away from the windows.
今すぐ外に出ろ！	Get outside right now!
倒れそうな家具のそばから離れてください	Please stay away from furniture that may fall.
そこ、カップが割れているから、気をつけて	There's a broken cup there, so be careful.
テレビで最新の地震情報を確認しましょう	Let's watch the earthquake updates on TV.
煙草の火を消してください	Please put out your cigarette.
念のため、窓やドアを開けて出口を確保しておきましょう	Just in case, let's open the windows and doors for easy evacuation.
ガスの元栓を閉めてください	Please turn off the gas.

安全を確認する

何か壊れてしまったものはありませんか？	Has anything broken?
床や天井にひびは入っていませんか？	Are there any cracks in the floor or ceiling?
ドアは開きますか？	Does the door open?
コンロの火が消えているか確認してください	Please make sure that the burners on your stove are off. ☑ 最初の揺れが収まってから、火元の確認をすることが推奨されています。
ほかの部屋も問題がないか確認してきてもらえますか？	Could you go check that everything is fine in the other rooms?

エレベーター内にいた場合

すぐにすべての階のボタンを押してください	Push the buttons for all floors immediately. ☑ 停止した階ですぐに降りるのがよいとされています。
緊急停止したみたいです	It looks like there was an emergency stop.
またすぐに動き出すはずです	It should start moving again soon.
そのボタンを押せば、外部に連絡できますよ	You can reach outside lines by pushing that button.
エレベーターは落下したりしません	The elevator won't fall down the shaft.

小〜中規模の災害

地震に対応する（屋外）

▶具体的な行動を指示する

建物から離れてください	Please stay away from the building.
そこの看板が落ちてくる可能性がありますよ	There is a possibility that sign over there may fall off.
電柱・ブロック塀・自動販売機などには近づかないように	Please stay away from electric poles, concrete block fences and vending machines.
かばんで頭を保護してください	Protect your head with your bag.
離れず、一緒に行動してください	Please stay together.
車に気をつけてください	Please watch out for cars.
警官の指示に従ってください	Please follow the officer's instructions.
とりあえず、駅に向かいましょう	To begin with, let's make our way to the station.
向こうの道は液状化していて危険です	Due to the soil liquefaction, the street over there has become a danger zone.
（携帯電話やスマホで）地震情報をチェックしてくれる？	Can you check your phone for earthquake updates?

地下にいた場合

地下街のほうが、かえって安全かもしれませんよ	It may be safer underground.
場内放送を聞いてみよう	Let's listen to the announcements.
非常口の位置を確認しよう	Why don't we check where the emergency exits are?
このまましばらく地下にとどまって、様子を見よう	Let's keep still for a while here underground and see what happens.
非常階段から、地上に出よう	Let's get out to the street using the emergency stairway.

海岸や川岸にいた場合

海岸から離れてください	Keep away from the coast.
津波が来る可能性がありますよ	It's possible that a tsunami will hit.
高い場所に逃げてください	Please escape to higher ground.
念のため、あの建物の中で待機しよう	Just to be safe, let's wait inside that building.
（海の中にいる人に対して）水から上がってください	Please get out of the water.
川で起こる津波に注意してください。大きな波が逆流して発生します	Be careful of river tsunamis. They happen when large waves travel upstream.

地震に対応する（自動車）

▶具体的な行動を指示する

左側に寄せて駐車しましょう	Let's pull over to the left.
救急車に道を譲って	Make way for the ambulance to get through.
消防車に道を譲って	Let the fire engine pass us.
高速道路を下りたほうがいいかもしれないね	It's probably best if we get off the highway.
交差点では特に気をつけて運転してください	Drive carefully when you reach an intersection.
トンネルから出よう	Let's get out of the tunnel.
ラジオで交通情報を聞きましょう	Let's listen to the traffic report on the radio.

▶状況を説明してあげる

この先の道は通行止めです	The road ahead is blocked.
ここから10キロの渋滞だそうです	Traffic is backed up for 10 kilometers ahead.
高速の入り口は封鎖されています	The entrance to the highway is closed.

地震に対応する（電車）

▶ 具体的な行動を指示する

手すりにつかまって！	Hold onto the rail.
電車の走行中はむやみに動かないで座っていて。	Please remain seated while the train is in motion.
乗務員の指示に従いましょう	Let's follow the crew's instructions.
指示があるまで車外に出てはいけません	Do not exit until you have been instructed to do so.
線路脇には高圧電線があるので、感電の恐れがあります	There is a danger of exposure to high-voltage cables on the side of the tracks.

状況を説明してあげる

電車が緊急停止するよ	The train will make an emergency stop.
すぐに動き出すよ	It'll start moving again soon.
今、安全確認をしているそうです	It looks like they're conducting a safety check at the moment.
待つしかないね	All we can do is wait.
地下鉄は思っているよりずっと安全なんですよ	The subway is much safer than you think.

▶駅構内にいた場合

地震で電車が止まっているよ	The trains have stopped due to the earthquake.
電車が動いていないからタクシーに乗ろうか	The trains aren't running, so shall we take a taxi?
電車はしばらく動きそうもないよ	It seems like the trains won't be running for a while.
駅員に話を聞いてみるね	Let me ask a member of the station staff.
ホームは混雑しているから、改札の外で待ったほうがいいですよ	The platforms are packed, so we should wait outside the gates.
隣の駅まで歩けば電車に乗れますよ	You can take the train if you walk to the next station.
電車は動いていませんが、バスは平常運行しています	The train isn't running, but the bus is running as usual.
しばらく復旧しそうもないので、外に出ませんか？	It doesn't seem it will be moving again for a while, so do you want to go outside?
小田急線ではJR線への振替輸送を実施しているそうです。駅員から振替輸送票をもらいましょう	The Odakyu Line is transferring passengers to the JR lines. Let's get a free transfer ticket from the station staff.
遅延証明書を発行しているようです	It seems they are giving out delay certificates.

▶火災に気づいた場合

火事だ！	It's a fire!
煙が出てるぞ	I see smoke.
何か焦げくさいな	It smells like something's burning.
ごみ箱から火が出てる	There's fire coming from the trash bin.
火元はキッチンだ	The fire is in the kitchen.
火を消せ！	Put out the fire!
119番に電話して	Call 119!
爆発音がしたぞ！	It sounds like something exploded!
火災報知器が鳴ってる！	The fire alarm is ringing!
非常ベルを鳴らして！	Push the fire alarm!
隣の家が燃えてる！	The house next door is on fire!
車が炎上しているぞ！	The car is in flames!
あそこの人たちを避難させよう！	Let's evacuate those people over there!

逃げろ！	Run!
非常口はあっちだ！	The emergency exit is over there!
煙を吸わないようにして！	Try not to inhale any smoke! ☑ inhale はインヘイルと発音します。
姿勢を低くして	Stay low.
防火扉を全部閉めて	Close all fire doors.
落ち着いて非常階段でおりましょう	Let's stay calm and go down the fire escape.
これは訓練ではありません	This is not a drill.
避難ばしごを降ろして	Lower the escape ladder.
ハンカチを口にあてて	Get a handkerchief and put it over your mouth.
手で口を覆って	Cover your mouth with your hand.
非常階段はそっちじゃない！ こっちだ！	The emergency stairs aren't over there! They're over here!
下の階はもう火が回っている。屋上に行こう！	The downstairs is already on fire. Let's head up to the roof!
服に火が燃え移ったら、動きを止め、床に寝て、左右に転がりましょう	If your clothes catch fire, stop, drop and roll. ☑ アメリカなどでは、火災時の安全対策として、この stop, drop and fall という動きを、子供たちに教えています。

火を消すのを手伝って	Help me put out the fire.
誰か消火器を取ってきて	Somebody go get the fire extinguisher.
毛布を使って火を消そう	Let's put the fire out with a blanket.
バケツに水を汲んできて	Go and bring back a bucket of water.
人を集めてバケツリレーをしよう	Let's gather everyone here and do a bucket brigade.
燃えやすいものを遠ざけよう	Let's take flammable items away from the fire.
ちゃんと火が消えたかどうか確認しよう	Let's check whether the fire has died or not.
消火器の使い方は、わかる？	Do you know how to use a fire extinguisher? ☑「消火器の使い方」は p.210 を参照
後は消防隊に任せよう	Let's leave the rest to the firefighters.
消火栓を使って火を消そう	Let's use the fire hydrant to put out the fire. ☑「屋内消火栓の使い方」は p.216 を参照
他にも燃えているところがないか確認しよう	Check if other areas are burning.

小〜中規模の災害

安否確認をする

▶行方不明者がいないか確かめる

全員そろってますか？	Do we have everyone?
サリーさんは、どこにいますか？	Where's Sally?
ボブさんが見当たりませんが、誰か知りませんか？	We can't find Bob. Does anyone know where he is?
ロンさん、加藤さんがどこにいるか確認してください	Hey Ron, please try to find Mr. Kato.
ソーニャさん、いませんか？ 返事をしてください	Sonya, are you here? Can you hear me?

▶無事かどうか確認する

ケガはない？	Any injuries?
火傷をした人はいませんか？	Did anybody get burned?
みんな、大丈夫？	Is everyone okay?
気分のすぐれない人はいませんか？	Anyone not feeling well?
手助けの必要な人はいませんか？	Anyone need help?
体調がよくないときは、すぐに知らせてくださいね	Please let us know right away if you don't feel well.

情報を収集する

交通機関について

中央線は動いていますか？	Is the Chuo Line running?
丸ノ内線に遅れは出ていますか？	Are there any delays on the Marunouchi Line?
梅田行きのバスは走っていますか？	Is the bus to Umeda in service?
この辺りでタクシーをつかまえられますか？	Can I catch a cab somewhere around here?
飛行機に遅れは出ていますか？	Are there any flight delays?
通行止めになっている道路はありますか？	Are there any dead end roads?

ライフラインについて

千葉市は停電していますか？	Is there a power outage in Chiba City?
ガスは止まっていませんか？	Has the gas stopped?
水道は使える？	Is the tap working?
ネットはつながるの？	Can you connect to the Internet?
発電機はありますか？	Do you have a power generator?

これは何のサイレンですか？	What's that siren for?
太平洋岸に津波注意報は出ていますか？	Is there a tsunami advisory for the Pacific coast? ☑ 警報・注意報については p.220 を参照してください。
大津波警報が出ているのはどの辺りですか？	What areas are under a severe tsunami warning?
津波警報は解除されましたか？	Have they canceled the tsunami warning?

▶その他

震源地はどこだったんですか？	Where was the epicenter?
長野県の被害状況について何か知ってる？	Do you know anything about the damage in Nagano Prefecture?
ここは津波の危険はありますか？	Is there any danger of a tsunami here?
津波の被害は出ているの？	Was there any damage from the tsunami?
この建物は安全ですか？	Is this building safe?
ミウラスーパーは営業していますか？	Is Miura Supermarket open?

震源は千葉県北部 のようですよ	The earthquake epicenter seems to have been in the northern part of Chiba Prefecture.
震源の深さはおよ そ150キロです	The depth of the epicenter was about 150 kilometers.
さっきの地震で は、愛知県では まったく揺れな かったそうですよ	I heard that the earthquake didn't affect Aichi Prefecture at all.
さっきの地震によ る津波の心配はな いそうです	They say that there is no danger of a tsunami from the earthquake earlier.
地震の影響で、明日 の朝、日本にも津波 が押し寄せる可能 性があります	Due to the earthquake, there is a possibility of a tsunami hitting Japan tomorrow morning.
この地域における 津波の到達予想時 刻は午後1時ごろ で、予想される最 大波の高さは40 センチだそうです	The tsunami is expected to hit this area at about 1:00 pm, and the estimated height is 40 centimeters.
安全が確認される まで、列車の運行 を一時取りやめる そうです	The trains will be temporarily stopped until safety checks are finished.
テレビをつけてみ て。地震速報が流 れるはずです	Turn on the TV. Information on the earthquake is supposed to air.

Chapter 3

大規模災害

大きな揺れを感じたら

▶地震に対する反応

大きいぞ	It's a strong one.
かなり大きい地震だぞ	It's a really strong earthquake.
いったいいつまで揺れるんだろう	How long is it going to shake?
避難したほうがいいかも	Maybe we should escape.
ここから出よう	Let's get out of here.
着替えている時間はない！ 行くぞ！	There's no time to change clothes! Let's go!
こんなに大きな揺れははじめてだ	I've never felt such intense shaking.
この建物は大丈夫かな？	Will this building be okay?
立っていられない	I can't keep my balance.
揺れがひどくて、酔ってしまいそうだ	It's shaking so hard that I'm starting to feel sick.
直下型だ！	It's coming from right below us! ☑「真下から来ているぞ」が直訳。
まだ死にたくない！	I don't want to die!

声をかける

落下物に気をつけろ	Watch out for falling objects.
外に飛び出すな！	Don't run out!
窓から離れて！	Stay away from windows!
必ず揺れはおさまるよ	Eventually, the shaking will stop.
パニックにならないで	Don't panic.
身の回りの物は置いて、とにかく逃げよう！	Leave your things and let's go!

危険を知らせる

危ない！ あの木、倒れるぞ！	Watch out! That tree will fall.
地割れが起こったぞ	The ground cracked.
割れたガラスが降ってくるぞ！	Watch above you for broken glass!
天井が崩れてくるぞ！	The roof's going to cave in! ☑ cave in「崩壊する」
車が突っ込んでくるぞ！	That car's going to crash into here!
橋が落ちそうだ	It looks like that bridge is going to collapse.
あのビルの外壁が崩れそうだ	It looks like the walls of that building will crumble.

大地震発生直後の対応を指示する（場所別）

▶ 集合住宅など（管理人からの指示）

指示があるまで、自分の部屋で待機してください	Please remain in your rooms until instructions are given.
断水するかもしれないので、水道水を蓄えておきましょう	The water may stop, so let's start storing some away.
この建物は耐震設計なので、倒壊の恐れはありません	This is an earthquake-resistant building, so it's not in danger of collapsing.
停電で廊下の電気が消えているので、ご注意ください	Due to the power outage, the lights in the hallways are off, so please be careful.
再通電に備えて、すべての暖房機器の電源を切っておいてください	In preparation for when the power comes back on, please turn off all heaters.
建物が倒壊する恐れがあるので、外に出てください	The building might fall down, so please exit the building.
エレベーターは停電のため、停止しています	Due to the blackout, the elevator is stalled. ☑ 複数のエレベーターがある場合は、elevators a▮ となります。
お風呂の水を抜かずにおくと、いざというとき便利です	Always keeping your bathtub full of water can come in handy in a crisis.

エレベーターは使わないでください	Please do not use the elevator(s).
別途指示があるまで、机の下に身を隠していてください	Please stay under your desks until further instructions are given.
帰宅するより、オフィスに泊まるほうが安全ですよ	Rather than going home, it's safer to spend the night in the office.
総務課の防災担当者の指示に従ってください	Please follow the instructions of the General Affairs Division Safety Officer. ☑ safety officer は「安全管理者」のことで、「緊急時に動いてリーダーになる者」のことを指します。
サンホテルに5部屋空きがあるそうです。希望者は、申し出てください	I was informed that they have five rooms available at Sun Hotel. If you'd like to book one, please let me know.
被害状況を報告してください	Please be sure to file a damage report.
ヘルメットを着用し、待機していてください	Please be sure to wear a helmet and remain on standby.
各課の課長は、課員の安全を確認後、総務に報告してください	All departmental managers, please report to General Affairs after confirming the safety of your staff.
薬剤などの危険物がこぼれていないかチェックしてください	Please make sure that no solutions or other hazardous materials have spilled.

商品棚から離れてください	Please stay away from display cases.
広いスペースにいたほうが安全です	It's safer to stay in bigger spaces
正面出入り口に人が殺到しています。他の出口に回ってください	The main entryway is crowded at the moment. Proceed to other exits.
避難口誘導灯に従って、非常口を目指してください	Please follow the warning lights leading to the emergency exit.
順番を守ってください	Please stay in order.
防火シャッターが自動的に閉まりますので、気をつけてください	The fire shutters close automatically, so please use caution.
当ビルは耐震設計になっていますので、倒壊の危険はございません	This building is earthquake resistant, so it's not in danger of collapsing.
天井からの落下物にご注意ください	Please watch out for objects falling from the ceiling.
地震のため停電していますが、まもなく非常灯がつくはずです	There's been a power outage due to the earthquake, but the emergency lights should come on soon.

ヘルメットをかぶってください	Please wear a helmet.
慌てずに校庭に移動しましょう	Let's move to the schoolyard in an orderly fashion. ☑ in an orderly fashion「秩序を保った状態で」という意味の言い回しです。
私の指示に従ってください	Please follow my instructions.
机の下に隠れて、頭を保護しなさい	Please get under your desks and cover your heads.
防災頭巾をかぶりなさい	Put on your disaster hoods.
ケガをした人は、申し出てください	Please report to us if you get hurt.

屋外で

海岸や河川から離れてください	Please keep away from coasts and rivers.
お子さんの手をしっかり握ってあげてください	Please hold on to your child's hand.
ここは安全そうなので、揺れが収まるまでじっとしていましょう	This looks like a safe place, so let's stay here until the shaking stops.
車道に飛び出さないでください	Please do not run into the street.
車から降りてください	Please get out of the car.
私についてきてください	Please follow me.

大規模災害

大地震による被害・二次災害について注意を促す

▶ 屋内の場合

この建物はいつ倒壊してもおかしくありません	This building may collapse any minute now.
この部屋の窓は割れているので、入らないでください	The windows in this room are broken, so please do not enter.
ものが床に散乱しているので、靴を履かずに入らないでください	Many things are scattered all around the floor, so please don't go without your shoes on.
階段が崩れかけているので、注意しましょう	The staircase is starting to give out, so let's be careful. ☑ give out「壊れる、ダメになる」
余震に備えて、落ちそうなものは降ろしておきましょう	Keeping the possibility of aftershocks in mind, let's take down anything that may fall.
避難することを考えたほうがいいかもしれません	We should really consider evacuating.
ドアがちゃんと開閉するかどうか確かめてください	Please check if the door still opens and shuts.
照明が落ちてくるかもしれないので、気をつけてください	The lights may fall down, so please be careful.
壊れた棚の角が尖っていて危険です	The sharp edges on the broken shelf are dangerous.

割れた窓ガラスに注意して歩いてください	Please watch out for broken glass while walking.
地割れの起きているところがあります	There are some spots with cracks in the ground.
地割れに落ちないように気をつけて	Be careful not to fall into the cracks in the ground.
ガラスが落ちてくるので、その建物には近づかないで	There's glass falling from the building, so don't go near it.
電線がたるんでいるところがあるので、頭上に注意してください	Electric cables are loose in some areas, so please look above your head.
信号が壊れているので、道路を渡るときは気をつけてください	The traffic lights are out, so please use caution when crossing the street.
切れた電線には絶対に触らないで	Do not touch broken electric cables.
あの電信柱は今にも倒れそうなので十分気をつけてください	That telephone pole may fall over anytime, so please be extra careful.
水道管が破裂して、水が噴き出しています。気をつけて	A water pipe broke, and water's gushing everywhere. Be careful.

大規模災害

揺れがおさまったので、ガスの元栓を閉めてください	The shaking stopped, so please shut off the gas.
ストーブやその他の暖房器具の電源を抜いてください	Please unplug all heaters and other heating appliances.
ろうそくは倒れて危険なので、懐中電灯を使いましょう	Candles can fall over and cause more danger, so let's only use flashlights.
ろうそくを使用する場合は、目を離さないように	If you use a candle, keep your eye on it.
近くで山火事が発生したので、いつでも避難できる準備をしてください	A forest fire started on the mountain nearby, so be ready to evacuate at any time.
ガス漏れの可能性があるので、火は使わないでください	There's a possibility the gas is leaking, so please don't use fire.
念のため、ブレーカーを落としましょう	Just to be safe, let's shut off the electricity.
タバコを吸うなんて、もってのほかですよ	Smoking is completely out of the question. ☑ out of the question「問題外で」

遠くではなく、高いところに逃げてください	Rather than trying to go far, please escape to higher ground.
津波は低くても十分危険なんですよ	A small tsunami is still a great danger.
最悪の事態に備えて、高台に行きましょう	Let's prepare for the worst and go somewhere high.
津波警報は出ていませんが、念のため避難することを考えましょう	No tsunami warnings have been issued, but we should think about evacuating just to be safe.
津波は繰り返し押し寄せるので、油断しないように	A tsunami strikes more than once, so we have to be careful.
潮が引き始めているから、津波がくるかもしれません	The tide is receding, so a tsunami may be approaching.
揺れがかなり大きかったので、津波が発生するかもしれません	It shook pretty hard, so it may cause a tsunami.
万が一津波が来た場合に備えて、この建物の屋上に上っておきましょう	In case a tsunami comes, let's get on the roof of this building.

大規模災害

台風による被害への対応を指示する・注意を促す

▶ 水害（浸水、冠水など）

このままでは床上浸水する可能性もあります	If the water keeps coming in, there's a possibility of above-floor-level flooding.
土嚢を今のうちに用意しておきましょう	We should get the sandbags ready now.
冠水した車のエンジンをかけるのは危険です	It's dangerous to start a car that has been submerged.
フロントガラスではなく、側面のガラスを割って脱出して！	Break the side windows, not the windshield, and escape through those. ☑ 側面のガラスのほうが割れやすくなっています。

▶ 土石流・崖崩れ・地すべり

裏山が崖崩れを起こす危険性があります	There is the danger of a landslide on the mountain behind us.
崖崩れが起きたら、この家は倒壊する恐れがあります	If there is a landslide, this house is in danger of being destroyed.
地鳴りが聞こえる！	The ground is rumbling!
湧き水が濁っている！	The spring water is muddy. ☑ 「湧水の濁り」は、「鉄砲水の前兆」とされています。
斜面に亀裂ができている！	The slope is cracking.

暴風

風が強くて危険なので、絶対に外に出ないでください	High winds are dangerous, so please do not go outside.
立っていられないほどの強い風が吹いています	The winds are so strong that you can't stand up.
飛来物でケガをする可能性がありますよ	Flying debris can cause injury.
家を補強しておいた方がいいですよ	You should reinforce your house.
もうすぐここも風速25メートル以上になります	In moments, wind speeds will surpass 25 meters per second. ☑ surpass「…を超える」

河川の氾濫

川には近づかないように	Do not go near rivers.
橋は倒壊の危険があるので、渡らないように	The bridge is in danger of collapsing, so do not cross it.
多摩川の堤防が決壊したようです	It seems that the levee of the Tama River has collapsed.
ダムが放水するかもしれないので、川岸から離れてください	The dam may release water, so please stay away from the river bank.
雨が止んだ後も、しばらく水位は高いままなので、注意が必要です	We must be cautious even after the rain stops because water levels remain high for some time.

避難する

▶ 避難の指示をする（地震や台風の場合）

警察から避難指示がありました	The police have instructed us to evacuate.
消防署から避難勧告がありました	The fire department has put out an evacuation advisory.
一刻も早く、ここから避難して！	Evacuate this place immediately!
家が倒壊する危険があるので、避難しましょう	The house is in danger of collapsing, so let's evacuate.
津波の危険があるので、今すぐ逃げよう	There's a tsunami risk, so let's leave right now.
余震が来るかもしれないので、ここから避難しよう	There may be aftershocks, so let's get out of here.
落石や地滑りが起こりそうだから、この場を離れよう	There's a threat of rockfalls and landslides, so let's get away from here.
雨風が強くなる前に、安全なところへ避難しよう	Let's find a safe place before the rain and winds get too strong.
高潮警報が発令されています	A storm surge warning has been issued. ☑ storm surge「高潮」
中川が氾濫寸前です。いますぐ避難して！	The Naka River is about to flood. Evacuate now!

貴重品は家に置いていかないように	Don't leave any valuables behind in your home.
どうしても必要なものだけを持っていきましょう	Let's only take the absolute necessities.
丈夫で動きやすい靴を履くように	Wear durable shoes that are easy to walk in.
留守の家族にはメモを残しておいてください	Please leave a message for family members who aren't home.
ガスの元栓を閉め、ブレーカーを落としてください	Please shut off the gas and electricity.
必要なものをまとめてください	Please gather all your necessities.
非常持ち出し袋を持ってきてください	Please bring your survival kit.
貴重品以外は、家に置いていってください	Aside from your valuables, please leave everything behind in your home.
懐中電灯を忘れずに持っていってください	Please remember to keep a flashlight with you.
避難の準備が出来たら、私に知らせてください	When you are ready to evacuate, please let me know.

非常口はこの先です	The emergency exit is just up ahead.
直ちに外に出てください	Please exit the premises immediately.
外の駐車場に一時避難してください	Please take refuge temporarily in the parking lot outside.
建物から出た後は、広域避難場所である東公園に移動してください	Once you have evacuated the building, please go to the Regional Evacuation Site at Higashi Park.
この建物は古いため、老朽化しているかもしれません。気をつけて避難してください	This building is very old, so may be damaged. Please be careful when evacuating.
慌てず、階段で避難してください	Please stay calm and use the stairs to evacuate.
非常階段は、この先を左に曲がったところにあります	Turn left ahead, and you'll find the fire escape.
防火扉は手動で開けられるので、そこから簡単に外に出られます	The fire door can be opened manually, so you can easily get outside.
渡り廊下を通って、隣の建物に移動してください	Please use the skybridge to cross over to the next building.

避難はしごを下ろしてください	Please let down the emergency escape ladder.
非常階段で下に降りよう	Let's go down the fire escape.
救助袋を下ろして！	Get the escape chute ready!
早く脱出用シューに入りなさい	Quickly get into the evacuation chute.
非常用すべり台で、校庭に避難しましょう	Let's escape into the schoolyard using the evacuation slide.
緩降機を使って、地上に降りましょう	Let's use the emergency descent rope to get down to ground level. ☑「緩降機」とは、高いところからゆっくり安全に降下するための、滑車つきロープのこと。descending lifeline とも言います。
避難ばしごは、この箱に収納されています	The emergency escape ladder is stored in this box.
誰か、避難ばしごを下ろすのを手伝ってください	Please, somebody, help me let down the emergency escape ladder.
非常用すべり台を使って、1階に降りましょう	Let's use the emergency evacuation slide to get down to the first floor.
下に見えるエアクッションに飛び降りてください！真ん中の白い円に向かって、足から飛び降りて！	Please jump onto the air cushion down there. Try to fall feet-first aiming towards the round, white part in the middle.

大規模災害

最寄りの避難所までは、歩いて10分ぐらいですよ	The nearest evacuation center is about a 10-minute walk from here.
3丁目の中川小学校が避難所です	Nakagawa Elementary School on City Block 3 is an evacuation center.
大石中学校へ向かおう	Let's go to Oishi Middle School.
避難場所への行き方はわかりますか？	Do you know how to get to the evacuation site?
この坂をまっすぐ上れば、左手に避難所の平和公園があります	Go straight up this hill. You will see the Evacuation Site at Heiwa Park on your left.
建物が崩れていて進めないから、他の道を通ろう	A building collapsed and is blocking this street, so let's take a different one.
富士見公園より、秀名大学のほうが安全ですよ	Shumei University is safer than Fujimi Park.
避難所の場所は少しわかりにくいので、私が連れて行ってあげますよ	The Evacuation Site is a bit difficult to find, so I'll take you there.
避難所は少し遠いですが、頑張って歩きましょう	The Evacuation Center is a bit far, but let's walk there.
避難所まではあと少しですよ！	Just a little further and we'll be a the Evacuation Site.

高台へ逃げて！	**Run to higher ground!**
この建物の屋上に行くのが安全です	**We'll be safe if we get on the roof of this building.**
すぐそこまで来てるぞ！	**It's going to hit!**
死にたくなかったら走れ！	**Run if you don't want to die!**
あそこの建物の屋上に避難しよう	**Let's evacuate to the roof of that building over there.**
津波避難タワーに登ろう	**Let's climb up the tsunami evacuation tower.** ☑ 津波避難タワーとは、数メートルから数十メートルの高さがある鉄骨製のタワーで、津波の際に上って津波をやりすごすためのものです。
そこの公園に、津波避難タワーが設置されています	**A tsunami evacuation tower has been set up in the park over there.**
津波は川を逆流してくるので、急いで川岸から離れましょう	**The tsunami could reverse water flow, so please get away from the banks immediately.**
そっちに逃げたらダメだ！	**Don't run that way!**
あの坂を上って！	**Climb the hill!**
もう間に合わない！ その電信柱につかまれ！	**We won't make it! Hold on to the telephone pole.**

大規模災害

姿勢を低くしたまま逃げて	Stay low and get out.
煙を吸わないように、口を覆って	Cover your mouth and try not to inhale any fumes. ☑ inhale はインヘイルと発音します。
隣の家が火事なので、今すぐ避難してください	The house next door is on fire, so please evacuate immediately.
風上に逃げよう	Let's run upwind.
火災旋風だ！川に飛び込め！	It's a firestorm! Jump into the river! ☑ 火災旋風とは、大規模な火災時に発生する、竜巻のような空気の渦のこと。関東大震災や東京大空襲の際、大規模に発生し、甚大な被害をもたらしました。
中に戻っちゃダメだ！	Don't go back inside! ☑ 燃えている建物の中に戻ろうとしている人に対して。
1つ上の階が燃えているので、急いで下の階から逃げましょう	The floor above is on fire, so let's hurry downstairs and get out.
廊下は火の海です。窓から救助を求めるしかありません	The hallways are in flames. Our only option is to call out for help from the window.
飛んでくる火の粉に気をつけて！	Watch out for sparks.
その建物は焼け落ちそうだから、今すぐに離れて！	That building looks like it will burn down, so get away!

車を置いて逃げましょう	Let's leave the car and run away.
車を置いていくなら、通行の妨げになったときに移動できるように、エンジンキーを付けたままにしてください	If you abandon your car, leave the key in so it can be moved easily when obstructing traffic.
窓は閉めましたか？	Did you close the windows?
貴重品を車においたままにしてはいけませんよ	Don't leave your valuables behind in the car.
連絡先のメモを残しておいたら？	Why don't you leave a note with your contact information?
車検証を持っていったほうがいいよ	Keep your vehicle inspection certificate on you.
ドアをロックしないように	Do not lock the doors.
［高速道路で］トンネルにも非常口があるので安心して	Tunnels also have emergency exits, so don't worry.
車より、命のほうがずっと大切だよ	Your life is far more precious than your car.
消火栓をふさがないように駐車してください	Please don't block the fire hydrant with your car.

施設や交通機関のスタッフからの指示

▶警官・警備員

警官の誘導に従ってください	Please follow the officers' instructions.
しばらくそのままでお待ちください	Please wait here for the time being.
指示するまで、その場を動かないでください	Please do not move until we give you instructions.
信号が故障しているので、警官の指示に従ってください	The traffic lights are broken, so please follow the officers' instructions.
立ち止まらないでください	Move along, please.
広域避難所のさくら公園へ移動してください	Please make your way to the Regional Evacuation Site at Sakura Park.
自動車は使わないでください	Please do not use cars.
押し合わないで、落ち着いて行動してください	Please proceed calmly and do not push.
迷子がいたら、教えてください	Please let us know if you find any lost children.
ベッキーちゃんのお母さんはいませんか？	Is Becky's mother here?

走らないでください	Please do not run.
押さないでください	Please do not push.
子供、お年寄り、女性の順番でシューターを使って降りてください	Go down the chute in the following order: children, the elderly then women.
消火作業にご協力ください	Please help with fire-fighting operations.
外の駐車場に避難してください	Please evacuate to the parking lot outside.
落ち着いて、外に避難してください	Please stay calm and go outside.
エレベーターは停止しています	The elevators are stopped.
避難の手助けが必要な方はおっしゃってください	If anyone needs assistance evacuating, please speak up.
館内で火災が発生しました。火元は2階の宴会場です。落ち着いて避難してください	A fire has broken out on the premises. The fire is in the banquet hall on the second floor. Please remain calm and evacuate the building.
各階廊下の突き当たりから、非常階段を利用できます	Please use the fire escape stairs at the end of the hallway on all floors.

大規模災害

駅舎が倒壊する恐れがあるので、中に入らないでください	The train station is in danger of collapsing, so please do not go inside.
改札口を開放いたします	We will unlock the gates.
緊急停止します	The trains will make an emergency stop.
松戸駅で運行をとりやめます	This train will be out of service at Matsudo Station.
つり皮や手すりに、しっかりおつかまりください	Please hold on tight to the hanging straps and handrails.
非常コックを使って、ドアを開けてください	Please use the emergency door release switch to open the doors.
指示があるまで線路に降りないでください	Please do not go onto the tracks until instructed to do so.
ただいまから線路を歩いての移動を開始します	We will begin walking along the tracks now.
９号車で火災が発生しました	A fire has broken out in car 9.
博多駅まで歩いて避難します	We will walk to Hakata Station and seek refuge there.
振替輸送を実施しています	We are currently transferring passengers onto other trains.

お客様のなかに、お医者様はいらっしゃいますか？	Is there a doctor here?
3階で火災が発生しました	A fire has broken out on the third floor.
倒れる危険があるので、陳列棚から離れてください	The display case may fall over, so please step away.
前の方に続いて、落ち着いて非常口から出てください	Please remain calm and follow the person in front of you out the emergency exits.
買い物カゴはその場に置いて、急いで外に逃げてください	Please leave your shopping baskets and exit quickly.
出口はひとつではありません	There is more than one exit.
足元にお気をつけください	Please watch your step.
誘導灯に従って、落ち着いて避難してください	Please remain calm and escape by following the emergency lights.
ただちに屋上に避難してください	Please escape to the roof immediately.
現在消火作業中です	Fire-fighting operations are currently under way.

大規模災害

軽いケガをしている人や気分が悪い人などに対応する

▶ 具合をたずねる

大丈夫ですか？	Are you okay?
気分は悪くないですか？	Are you feeling alright?
お子さんの顔が真っ青ですが、大丈夫ですか？	Your child's face is pale, is he/she okay?
吐き気はありますか？	Do you feel nauseous? ☑ nauseous「吐き気のある」。「吐き気」は nausea。
顔色が悪いですよ	You're looking pale.
どこか痛みますか？	Does it hurt anywhere?
血が出ていますが、大丈夫ですか？	You're bleeding. Are you sure you're okay?
立てますか？	Can you stand upright?
避難所まで歩けますか？	Will you be able to walk to the Evacuation Center?
震えているようですが、大丈夫ですか？ 寒いですか？	You're shaking. Are you okay? Do you feel cold?
頭が痛いんですか？	Does your head hurt?
目はしっかり見えていますか？	Can you see okay?

腕は上がりますか？	Can you lift your arms?
人差し指を曲げてみてください	Please try bending your index finger.
ケガをしたのは腕だけですか？	Is your arm the only place you injured?
どんなふうに痛むんですか？	What kind of pain is it?
自分の名前を言えますか	Can you tell me your name?
どこが痛みますか？	Where does it hurt?
ケガしたところを見せてください	Show me your injury.

安静にさせる

仰向けで横になってください	Please lie down.
楽な姿勢を取ってください	Please get into a comfortable position.
ここに座ってください	Please sit here.
衣服を緩めてください	Please loosen your clothes.
日陰に入って横になってください	Please lie down in the shade.

大規模災害

消毒液を塗りますね	I'm going to rub some antiseptic on you now.
少ししみますよ	It will sting a bit.
このハンカチを傷口に当てて止血してください	Please use this handkerchief to cover the wound and stop the bleeding.
絆創膏を貼ってあげますね	I'll put a bandage over it now.
傷口をきれいに水で流しましょう	Let's wash and clean this wound with some water.
三角巾でひじを支えましょうか？	Shall we wrap a sling around you to support your elbow?
傷口を、心臓より高い位置に上げておいてください	Please raise the wound above chest-level. ☑ こうすると血が止まりやすくなります。
氷で冷やしましょう	Let's put some ice on it.
お子さんは過呼吸を起こしているようです。とにかく、落ち着かせましょう	Your child seems to be hyperventilating. Let's calm him/her down.
指が凍傷になりかけているので、温めましょう	You're starting to get frostbite in your fingers. Let's warm them up

階段から転げ落ちて、骨を折ったそうです	He/She fell down the stairs and broke a bone.
心臓に持病があるそうです	It seems like he/she has chronic heart disease.
高血圧の薬を常用しているそうです	It seems he/she is taking high blood pressure medication.
息が苦しいそうです	He/She is having trouble breathing.
ひどいめまいがするそうです	He/She is feeling very dizzy.
妊娠3か月だそうです	It seems like she is three months pregnant.
胃ではなく、下腹部が痛むそうです	He/she says it's not his/her stomach, but lower abdomen that is hurting.
薬物アレルギーがあるそうです	He/She is allergic to some medications.
ペースメーカーをつけているそうです	He/She is using a pacemaker.
転倒して頭をひどく打ったそうです	He/She fell down and hit his/her head badly.
ひどい吐き気がするそうです	He/She says he/she feels very nauseous.
かなり熱があるようです	He/She's running a fever.

大規模災害

人命を救助する

▶ 重傷者に声をかける

大丈夫ですか？ 肩を貸しましょう	Are you okay? You can lean on me.
ケガを治療してくれるところへ連れて行きましょうか？	Shall I take you somewhere to treat that injury?
ひどく痛みますか？ 痛み止めを飲まれますか？	Does it hurt really badly? Would you like a painkiller?
このぐらいの傷なら、大丈夫です。心配ありませんよ。	It's just a minor injury. You'll be okay. Don't worry.
必ず助かりますよ	I'm sure you'll be fine.
救急車を呼びますか？	Should we call an ambulance?
今、救急車を呼びましたよ	I just called an ambulance.
気をしっかり持って！ 今、助けが来ますからね！	Stay with me! Help is on the way. ☑ この Stay with me! は「気を確かに！」のように、意識を失いそうな人にかけるひとことです。
もうすぐ救助隊が来ますからね	The rescue team will be here soon.
医療スタッフが被害者の手首に付けている色のついたタグはトリアージタグと呼ばれるものです	The colored tags that medical personnel attaches to the victims' wrists are called triage tag. ☑ トリアージとは、多数の犠牲者が発生した大災害や事故の際、重症度に応じて、患者の治療の順序および優先度を決定するプロセスです。

重傷者の家族などに声をかける

お父さんは必ず助かりますよ	I'm sure your father will be okay.
AEDを使ってみます	We're going to use the AED.
お子さんの名前はなんですか？	What's your child's name?
今助けを呼んでいますから、声をかけ続けてください	We've called for help, so please keep talking.
お子さんは、藤井病院に搬送されるそうですよ	It looks like your child will be taken to Fujii Hospital.

逃げ遅れた人への声かけ

今助けを呼んだので、そこを動かないでください	I just called for help, so please stay here.
今、助けに行きますからね	I'm coming to help you now.
ロープか何かを探してきます	I'll go find a rope or something.
ヘリコプターが、そちらに救助に向かうそうです	The helicopter will go there to rescue you.
誰か人を呼んできます	I'll go and get somebody.

▶救急隊からの声かけ

今、そちらにはしごを延ばします	We will send a ladder down to you now.
(あなたを)担架に乗せますね	We're going to put you on the stretcher now.
あなたをおぶって運びます	I'll carry you on my back.
今、応急手当をしますからね	I'm going to give you first-aid now.
浮き輪を投げますので、それにつかまってください	We're going to throw you a lifesaver (ring), so hold on to it.

▶救助の手助けを頼む

この瓦礫の下に人がいます！	There are people under the debris!
このタンスを持ち上げるのを手伝ってください	Please help me lift this cabinet.
私がこちらの腕を支えるので、あなたは反対の腕を支えてあげてください	I'll hold this arm, so please hold the other arm.
意識を保つために、声をかけ続けてあげてください	Please keep talking to him/her, so he/she won't lose consciousness.
私1人では、この人を運べません。手伝ってもらえませんか？	I can't carry this person by myself. Can you help me?

この人を安全なところに移動させましょう	Let's take this person somewhere safe.
私が頭を持つので、あなたは足を持ってもらえますか？	I'm going to hold his/her head, so could you hold his/her legs?
この扉の向こうに何人か閉じ込められているようです	I think there are several people trapped on the other side of this door.
もっと人を集めてください	Please get more people.
背中をさすってあげてください	Please rub his/her back.

救助を求める

助けて！	Help!
救急車を呼んでもらえませんか？	Can you call an ambulance?
足をくじいてしまって、歩けないんです	I sprained my ankle and can't walk.
足が抜けないんです	My foot is stuck.
私を引っ張り上げてもらえませんか？	Can you pull me up?

▶ 人探しを手伝う

私も一緒に探しましょうか？	Shall I help you look for him/her?
ご主人は、どんな服を着ていましたか？	What was your husband wearing?
はぐれたときの状況を教えてください	Please tell me what was happening when you lost track of him/her. ☑ lose track of...「…を見失う」「…の行方がわからなくなる」
私はこっちのほうを探してみます	I'll go this way and search.
最後に息子さんを見たのは？	When's the last time you saw your son?
トーマス・サンダーソンさんという、男性を探しています。この子のお父さんなのですが…	I'm looking for a man named Thomas Sanderson. He's this child's father...
ミック君のお母さん、いませんか？	Is Mick's mother here/there?
ジョン・スミスさん、奥さんが探していますよ	Mr. John Smith, your wife is looking for you.
こちらの伝言板に、今いる避難先を書いたメモを貼っておくといいですよ	Please post a note with your current Evacuation Site's information on this bulletin board.
どこで姿が見えなくなりましたか？	Where did you lose track of him/her?

迷子探しを手伝う

トム君という5歳の男の子が迷子になっています	A five-year-old boy named Tom is missing.
ピンクのシャツを着た、3歳ぐらいの女の子を探しています	I'm looking for a three-year-old girl in a pink shirt.
お子さんを見かけた人がいないか、聞いてみますね	Let me ask around to see if anyone has seen your child. ☑ ask around「尋ねて回る」
私も一緒にお子さんを探しましょうか？	Shall I help you look for your child?
あなたの娘さんは、どんな服装をしていますか？	What was your daughter wearing?
このぐらいの背の高さの男の子を探しているのですが	I'm looking for a boy, about this tall.

迷子への声かけ

1人？ 大丈夫？	Are you alone? Are you okay?
お母さんかお父さんは、どこにいるの？	Where are your mother and father?
一緒にお母さんを探そうね	Let's find your mother.
大丈夫だから、泣かないでね	It's okay. Don't cry.
ママの名前はなんていうの？	What's your mother's name?

歳はいくつ？	How old are you?
どこから来たの？	What direction did you come from?
どこでお母さんとはぐれたの？	Where did you last see your mother?
お母さんかお父さんの携帯番号はわかる？	Do you know your mother or father's (cell) phone number?
家の住所を教えて？	Can you tell me your address?
あなたの名字は？	What's your last name?

▶ 見つかったことを報告する

キャシーちゃんが見つかりましたよ	We found Cathy.
カイル君は無事です。お母さんに会いたがっています	Kyle is safe. He says he wants to see his mother.
娘さんと思われる、3歳ぐらいの、水色のワンピースを着た女の子が保護されています	A three-year-old girl wearing a sky blue dress is being kept. She may be your daughter.
タニアちゃんが保護されている場所にお連れしましょう	Let me take you to where Tania is.
クリス君に似た子どもを見た人がいます。（その人に）会いに行きましょう	Someone saw a boy that looks like Chris. Let's meet him/her.

遺体確認や埋葬の手助けをする

遺体があることを知らせる

お住まいの地区で発見された遺体の多くは、名取小学校体育館に安置されているそうですよ	It looks like most of the bodies found in your area of residence are at Natori Elementary School's gym.
外国人と思われる方のご遺体は、ここに安置してあります	The bodies thought to be non-Japanese have been brought and are being kept here.
津波で亡くなった方の遺体が青島海岸に打ち上げられています	The bodies of those who were killed in the tsunami have washed onto the shores of Aoshima coast.
ご遺体は、ここでまなく、別の安置所にある可能性もありますよ	There is a possibility that the body you're looking for is not being kept at this center, but at a different morgue.
外国人とみられるたくさんのご遺体が、あの体育館に安置されていました	Many bodies of people thought to be non-Japanese were being kept in that other gym.
遺体の発見時の状況が書かれたカードが掲示されているので、それを元に探してください	Cards are on display that give details of where and how each body was found. Please use them as a reference when searching.
この小学校の校庭が、仮の遺体安置所になっています	The schoolyard of this elementary school is being used as a temporary morgue.
外国人とみられる、女の子の遺体が見つかったそうです	We've been informed that the body of a girl thought to be non-Japanese has been located.

▶遺体との対面

このご遺体は、あなたのお父さんで間違いありませんか？	Are you certain that this is your father's body?
こちらが、あなたの息子さんですね？	This body is your son's, right?
こちらの書式に、亡くなられた方のお名前とご住所をご記入ください	Please write the deceased person's name and address on this form.
サインをこちらにお願いいたします。	Please sign here.
こちらが、遺体発見時の所持品のリストになります	This is the list of the items found with the body.

▶遺体について説明する

記録によると、ご遺体は、北見駅のXYZビル付近で発見されました。	According to our records, he/she was found near the XYZ building right next to Kitami Station.
長時間海に浸かっていたため、遺体は激しく損傷しています	The body was under water for a long time, so it is badly damaged
このご遺体は、ビル火災で焼け出されたので、身元の確認が困難です	This body was recovered from a burning building, so identifying it may be difficult.
「品川XX-XX」の青いスポーツカーの中で、お亡くなりでした	He/She was found dead inside a blue sports car, license plate number "Shinagawa XX-XX."

このご遺体の身元を確認できるものは、見つかっていません	We couldn't find any identification on this corpse.
この財布が、旦那さんの上着のポケットに入っていました	This wallet was found inside your late husband's coat pocket.
私は旦那さんの最期に立ち会いましたが、「愛していると、妻に伝えてください」とおっしゃっていました	I was with your husband and his last words were, "Please tell my wife that I love her."

遺体の処理（埋葬・火葬）について説明する

災害緊急時の遺体処理規定で、お子様の遺体はこちらで火葬させていただきます	Following the regulations for the disposal of remains in emergency conditions, we will proceed to cremate your child's body on-site. ☑ cremate「…を火葬する」、on-site「その場で」
土葬に抵抗はあると思いますが、衛生上止むを得ない措置なので、ご理解ください	We understand that you are opposed to burial without cremation, but please understand that for health reasons, it is all we can do. ☑ burial without cremation「火葬なしでの埋葬」（つまり、土葬のこと）
云染病の蔓延を防ぐため、すべての遺体はこちらで土葬されます	In order to prevent the spread of infectious diseases, we must bury all the remains together on-site.
安置場所の不足のため、遺体はこちうで仮に埋葬し、後日改めて火葬処理をすることになります	Due to a shortage of morgues, we will hold funerals on-site, followed by cremations at a later date.

火葬が追いつかないため、すべての遺体は当地で2年を上限に仮埋葬（土葬）されるとのことです	Due to the large number of bodies awaiting cremation, all the remains will undergo temporary burial for up to two years.
これより、奥様のご遺体を埋葬いたします	We will now bury your late wife's body.
旦那さんの亡骸は、こちらの遺体収納袋に入れて、埋葬いたします	We will now bury your husband's remains in this body bag.
本国の方と連絡が取れますか？大使館に電話する必要がありますか？	Can you contact someone in your home country? Do you need to call the embassy?

▶ お悔やみの言葉をかける

心からお悔やみを申し上げます	I would like to offer you my deepest condolences.
奥様のご遺体に、お花をお供えさせてください	I'd like to give these flowers as an offering to your wife.
何か私にできることがあれば、おっしゃってくださいね	Please let me know if you need anything, anything at all.
私の父も津波で亡くなったので、あなたの気持ちはよくわかります	I also lost my father in a tsunami, so I understand how you must feel.

避難場所での声かけ

情報のやり取りをする

どこから避難してこられたんですか？	Where did you escape from?
三島町では、かなり地割れが発生していましたよ	There were large cracks in the ground in Mishima.
熊田町の被害規模は、どのようなものでしたか？	How great was the damage in Kumada?
3日間の総雨量が300ミリを超えたそうです	The total rainfall for those three days was over 300 millimeters.
明日も激しい雨が降り続くと聞きました	I heard that the heavy rain will continue through to tomorrow.

アドバイスする

回線がパンクしてしまうので、携帯電話の利用は最小限にしましょう	To avoid tying up the phone lines, please limit your cell phone use to the absolute minimum.
その建物の裏に、公衆トイレがありますよ	There's a public toilet behind that building.
そこのトイレに、おむつ交換台がありますよ	There's a diaper changing station in the restroom over there.
この水道の水は、飲用可能です	The tap water here is drinkable.

そこは立ち入り禁止ですよ	That area is off-limits. ☑ off-limits「立ち入り禁止の」
避難場所である、この公園内でタバコは吸えませんよ	Smoking is prohibited in this park, which now serves as an evacuation site.
お子さんが駆け回っています。危ないので、やめさせてください	Your children are running around. It's dangerous, so please make them stop.
その建物には入らないでください	Please do not enter that building.
敷地外に勝手に出ないでください	Please do not leave the premises without notice.

▶元気づける

お子さんはきっと見つかりますよ	I'm sure they will find your child.
希望を捨てないで	Never lose hope.
しばらくの辛抱です	Just be patient, everything will get better.
ご家族が無事でよかったですね	I'm so glad to hear your family is safe.
この避難所にいれば、ひとまずは安心ですね	For the time being, we are safe in this evacuation center.

帰宅困難者を助ける

職場の同僚にアドバイスする

交通機関が止まっているので、会社に泊まったほうがよさそうです	All mass transit is stopped, so we should stay here at the office.
お住まいは立川でしたっけ？ 歩いて帰るのは厳しいと思います	You live in Tachikawa, right? I think it's too far to walk from here.
JRは全線止まっているようです	It looks like all JR lines are out of service.
総務に行けば、毛布と非常食を提供してもらえますよ	You can get blankets and provisions from the General Office.
帰宅支援マップをチェックしてみましょう	Let's check the Emergency Commuter Map.

帰宅困難者への声かけ

お住まいは遠いんですか？	How far away do you live?
よかったら、私の家で少し休んでいきませんか	If you'd like, you can rest at my house for a bit.
水はいりますか？	Do you want some water?
道はわかりますか？	Do you know your way?

駅の近くの駐輪場で、自転車を貸し出していますよ	They're lending people bicycles at the bike-park near the station.
ここから博多駅までのバスならまだ運行していますよ	The bus from here to Hakata Station is still in service.
高円寺まで歩くと、3時間かかりますよ	It will take you three hours to get to Koenji.
遠回りでも、大通りを歩いたほうが安全です	Even if it's a longer distance, it's safer to walk on the big streets.
この先の大学の講堂で休めるそうです。毛布も貸し出しているそうですよ	You can rest at the auditorium of the university ahead. I heard they also provide blankets.
終電後も、その駅は「無料開放」を行っています	Even after the last train, you can stay in the station for free.
橋が崩れたため、この川は渡れないそうです	The bridge collapsed, so we cannot cross this river.
始発まであと2時間ほどですから、この駅で待った方がよさそうです	There are about two hours left until the trains start running, so it may be best to wait here at the station.
総武線は、運行を再開したそうです	They say that the Sobu Line has resumed service.

お金や犯罪に関すること

お金に関するアドバイスをする

停電のため、カードは使えないようですよ	Due to the power outage, it looks like we can't use credit cards.
両替してあげましょうか	Shall I change that bill for you?
小銭は持っていますか？	Do you have any change?
公衆電話を無料で使用できますよ	You can use the public payphone for free. ☑ 震災時は、公衆電話が無料で使えるようになります（国際電話は除く）
停電のため、銀行のATMは停止していると聞きました	I heard that the ATMs are down due to the blackout.

災害に伴う犯罪への注意

泥棒が留守宅を狙っているそうですよ	I heard thieves are targeting empty houses.
移動する際、貴重品は必ず携行してください	Please hold on to your valuables when moving from place to place.
留守宅に一人で戻るのは危険ですよ	It's very dangerous to return alone to an empty house.
バッグは肩に掛けるより、たすき掛けのほうがいいですね	It's better to put your purse across your body, rather than on your shoulder.
隣町で強盗被害があったそうです	There were reports of burglaries in the next town.

Chapter 4

避難所での生活と被災後の生活

避難所生活のルールを伝える

▶飲食・炊き出し

水の配給は、1人当たり1日3リットルです	The daily water ration is three liters per person.
不足する物資は、高齢者、障がい者、子ども、大人の順に配布します	If there is a shortage of supplies, they'll be distributed in the following order: the elderly, disabled, children then adults.
食器が不足しています。紙皿を含め、食器にはラップをかぶせて使用してください	There isn't enough tableware to go around, so please wrap all dishes, including paper plates, in plastic wrap and re-use them.
食事はお1人につき1人分だけお受け取りください	Each individual should take only one portion of food.
カップラーメンは1人2個まで、チョコレートなどの菓子類は3個までお受け取りいただけます	Each person is allowed two packages of cup ramen and three pieces of chocolate or candy.
朝食は、午前7時です	Breakfast is at 7:00 am.
夕食の配給は、午後6時からです	Dinner will be distributed starting at 6:00 pm.
使い終わった食器は、軽くゆすいだ後、所定の場所に持って行ってください	Once you are finished with your dishes, please rinse them off and take them to the designated area.
（調理に関わる人は）調理する前に必ず手を消毒してください	Please be sure to wash and disinfect your hands before preparing food.
飲酒は所定の場所でお願いします	Please drink alcohol only in the permitted areas.

外の簡易トイレを使ってください	Please use the portable toilets located outside.
みんなで使うので、トイレはきれいに使ってくださいね	We all use these bathrooms, so please keep them clean.
断水しているため、トイレは、このバケツの水を使って流してください	The water has been cut off, so use these buckets to flush the toilet.
トイレットペーパーの数が限られているので、節約してください	Toilet paper supplies are limited, so please be considerate.
便器にこの袋を取り付けてから、用を足してください。その後は凝固剤を入れて、袋の口を縛って破棄してください	Please affix this bag over the toilet bowl before using the bathroom. Be sure to add the coagulant and seal the bag tight before disposing of it.
断水のため、外にある仮設の汲み取り式トイレを使ってください	Due to the water outage, we are asking that you please use the latrines located outside.
詰まり防止のため、紙以外のものは流さないでください	To prevent clogging, do not flush anything other than toilet paper down the toilet.
手洗い・洗顔で使った水は、トイレ用水として使用するので、流して捨てないでください	The water used when washing your hands or face will be reused for flushing the toilet, so please do not flush it down the drain.
トイレの清掃は、みんなで交代で行います。時間は午前9時、午後2時、午後6時の3回です	We will take turns cleaning up the shelter bathrooms. The time slots are as follows: 9:00 am, 2:00 pm and 6 pm (three times/day).
清掃時間は放送でお知らせします	We will make an announcement when it's clean-up time.

入浴時間は 1 人 20分です	Use of the bath is limited to 20 minutes per person.
タオルをお持ちでない方は、申し出てください	Please let us know if you do not have a towel.
水不足のため、入浴は週に 1 回となっています。ご理解ください	Due to water limitations, we are limiting baths to once a week. We ask for your understanding.
タオルは浴槽に入れないでください	Do not bring your towels into the bathtub.
シャンプーや石けんは、浴室に置きっぱなしにしないでください	Do not leave shampoo, soap or other toiletries in the bath area.
シャワーを出しっぱなしにしないでください	Try not to leave the shower on.
先に体を洗ってから、浴槽に入ってください	Be sure to wash your body before getting into the bathtub.
乳幼児を入浴させたい親御さんのために、たらいを用意しています	We have wash bins available for parents who need to bathe their infants.
風呂場のそばのテントが脱衣所となっています。着替えはそこで行ってください	The tent next to the bathing room was set up as a changing room. Please go there to change clothes.
風呂を利用の際は、「入浴証」の提示が必要です。「入浴証」をお持ちでない方は有料となります	You must show your bathing pass before using the bath. Those without a pass will be charged a fee.

寝具

敷布団は1人1枚ずつです	Only use one futon mattress per person.
災害用エアーマットをベッド代わりに使ってください	Please use the emergency air mattress as a bed.
火事を避けるため、毛布は暖房器具から十分に離してください	To prevent fires, please be sure to keep your blankets a safe distance away from heating devices.
布団は敷きっぱなしにすると、ダニが発生するので、晴れた日は干しましょう	If futons are left out, they will attract mites. Let's hang them out on sunny days.
寝具の交換はお年寄りには重労働なので、若者が交代で行います	Changing bedding is hard work for the elderly, so we will have young residents do it in shifts.

ゴミの処理

ゴミはきちんと分別してください	Properly sort your trash.
ゴミはためこまずに、収集日に出してください	We ask that you not hoard trash and take it out on the scheduled collection days.
物品は再利用を心がけ、ゴミを増やさないようにしましょう	Please reuse items and don't produce large amounts of trash.
ペットボトルはラベルとキャップを外した上で、つぶして廃棄してください	Be sure to remove the labels and caps off plastic bottles before crushing and disposing of them.

紙おむつは、臭いが漏れないように、しっかりくるんでからビニール袋に入れて捨ててください	Tightly roll up dirty diapers to prevent the smell from spreading and put them in a plastic bag for disposal.
自分たちのゴミは、各世帯の責任で、敷地内のゴミ置き場に捨ててください	Each household is responsible for taking their own trash to the appropriate collection spots on the premises.
避難所内でのゴミの焼却は禁止です	Burning waste inside of the shelter is prohibited.
牛乳パックはかさばるので、つぶしてから捨ててください	Milk cartons are bulky, so flatten and fold them before discarding.
弁当の容器は、臭いを避けるため、軽く洗ってから燃えるゴミとして出してください	Please rinse food containers before discarding as burnable garbage to prevent odors.

▶ 洗濯

手回し式の洗濯機があるので、交代で使ってください	Hand laundry washers are available, so use them in turns.
来週には通常の洗濯機が届くそうです。それまでは手洗いをお願いします	A full-size washing machine will be coming in next week. Until then, please hand wash your laundry.
洗濯板があります。譲り合って使ってください	There are washboards available. Please try to share them.
関根川の水は飲用には適していませんが、洗濯には使えます	Water from the Sekine River is not for drinking but can be used for doing laundry.

喫煙

所定の喫煙スペースを除いて、全面禁煙です	With the exception of designated smoking areas, smoking is prohibited on the premises.
喫煙は、決められた喫煙スペースでお願いします	Please only smoke in the designated smoking areas.
吸殻は所定の容器に捨ててください	Please only dispose of cigarette butts in approved receptacles.
煙草は火が完全に消えたのを確認してから捨ててください	Please make sure cigarettes are completely out before disposal.
授業時間中、喫煙スペースは利用不可です	The smoking area is not available during school hours.

ペット

ペットは所定の場所につなぐか、ケージに入れましょう	Please keep your pets tied in the designated pet area or keep them locked in a cage.
フンの始末を常に行い、飼育場所を清潔にしましょう	Be sure to clean up after your pets at all times and keep the area around your pets clean.
施設を清潔に保つため、飼育場所は必要に応じて消毒してください	When necessary, please disinfect the area around your pets to keep the premises clean.
屋外で排便させ、後始末してください	Take your pets outside when they need to go to the bathroom and be sure to pick up after them.
餌やりは時間を決めて、その都度片付けてください	Set times to feed your pets and clean up after them.

散歩やブラッシングは、必ず屋外で行ってください	Please be sure to go outside when walking your pets or grooming them.
他人に迷惑がかからないようペットをしつけましょう	Make an effort to keep your pets in line so as not to bother others.
ペットと人とのトラブルを避けるよう努めてください	Make an effort to prevent any accidents involving your pets and other people.
ノミの駆除に努めてください	Take care of your pets' fleas.
あいにく、ここではペット禁止です	We're afraid we cannot allow pets on the premises.

▶ プライバシーに配慮する

プライバシー確保のために、段ボール製の間仕切りを用意しています	We have cardboard box dividers for your privacy.
更衣室として使えるよう体育館のステージの一画に囲いをしています	We have fenced off an area on the gym's stage to use as a changing room.
ご自身の区画から、荷物がはみ出さないようお願いします	We ask that you keep your belongings in your area.
家族単位で簡易テントをご利用ください	Each household is allowed use of a canopy.
お互いのプライバシーを尊重してください	We ask that everyone respect each others' privacy.

靴を脱いだら、必ず揃えてください	Be sure to tidy up your shoes after you take them off.
「立ち入り禁止」などの張り紙の指示には必ず従ってください	Pay attention and follow warning signs you see, such as "DO NOT ENTER."
消灯は午後9時。消灯後の会話はお控えください	Lights go out at 9:00 pm. Please refrain from talking after the lights go out.
この部屋での携帯電話の通話は禁止されています	Talking on mobile phones in this room is prohibited.
通話は、屋外や定められたスペースでのみ可能です	Talking on the phone is only allowed outside or in designated areas.
携帯電話はマナーモードに設定してください	Please keep your phones on silent mode.
周りの迷惑になりますので、大声で話すのはやめてください	Keep your voices down so as not to bother those around you.
裸火の使用は禁止です	The use of open flames is prohibited.
所定の場所以外での飲酒は禁止です	Alcohol consumption outside of the designated areas is prohibited.
必要な物資は、避難所の問い合わせ窓口に申し込んでください	Please submit any requests for personal necessities to the staff at the Shelter Help Desk.

避難所での生活と被災後の生活

在庫がある物はその場でお渡しします	We'll be distributing whatever we have in stock on the spot.
在庫にない物は本部へ要請しますので、詳細は問い合わせ窓口に来てください	Any supplies that are not in stock, we'll be requesting from the head office, so please come to the help desk for more information.
外来者は、入出場の際、受付での手続きが必要です	All outside visitors must sign in at the front before entering or leaving the premises.
当避難所は土足厳禁です	No outside footwear is allowed inside the premises.
先着順ではありません。世帯名を呼ばれたら、受付に来てください	It is not first-come, first-served. Please come to the front desk when we call your family up.
男性には、毎晩夜警を交代で行っていただきます	We ask that all men take turns being on night watch every night.
不審者を見つけたら、運営本部に連絡してください	If you spot any suspicious individuals, please report them to the head office.
許可なく掲示物を貼ったり、剥がしたりするのはやめてください	Do not post or remove postings from the bulletin board without permission.
外泊する場合は、事前に「外泊届用紙」を提出してください	Submit an "Overnight Absence Form" beforehand if you plan to spend the night off-premises.
食料の賞味期限に留意してください	Please be mindful of food expiration dates.

▶食事

この避難所には、200人が1か月過ごせる食料が備蓄されています	There is enough food to last 200 people one month in this shelter.
1人に1つずつ、カップラーメンが配給されるそうですよ	I hear that each person will be given one packet of cup ramen.
食料は公平に配給しているので、たとえ量が物足りなくてもご理解ください	Food is distributed equally to everyone, so please be understanding if portions are small.
昼食に、カレーライスが配給されます	Curry rice will be served for lunch.
あそこのカウンターのパンと飲み物は、ご自由にお取りください	Help yourself to the drinks and bread on the counter over there.
これは「けんちん汁」という食べ物ですよ	This is a food called Kenchin soup.
これは「アルファ米」と呼ばれ、水を入れるだけで調理できるんです	This is called Alpha rice. It is cooked by adding water.
この豚汁を食べれば体が温まります	This pork soup will warm you up.
明日、おにぎりの配給があります	Rationed rice balls will be available tomorrow.

避難所での生活と被災後の生活

スープが余っているので、お代わりが欲しい方はおっしゃってください	There is extra soup, so please let us know if you want more.
この料理には豚肉が使われています	This food contains pork.
この調味料には豚由来の原料が含まれています	This seasoning contains raw materials from pork.
緑茶にもカフェインは含まれています	Green tea also contains caffeine.
この肉は、ハラールフードではありません	This meat is not halal food. ☑ ハラールフードは「イスラム教の律法に則って処理をした食材」のこと。
遺伝子組み換え食品は使用していません	No genetically modified foods are used.
このスープには、ビーフエキスが含まれています	This soup contains beef extract.
これは米粉パンなので、小麦アレルギーの人でも大丈夫ですよ	This is rice bread, so people allergic to wheat can eat it.
このお菓子には、少量の海老が含まれています	These snacks contain a small amount of shrimp.
アナフィラキシーショックを防ぐため、アレルギーのある方は申し出てください	To avoid anaphylactic shock, please tell us if you have any allergies.
食べられない食材を言っていただければ、あなた用の食事を別に用意しますよ	Tell us what ingredients you can't eat and we will prepare a separate meal for you.

トイレ

簡易トイレは水洗ではありません	The portable toilet does not flush with water.
トイレを我慢するのは体によくありませんよ	Holding out on using the toilet is bad for your body.
トイレットペーパーは、この棚にストックされています	Toilet paper is stored on this shelf.
2階にもトイレがあるので、1階のトイレが混んでいる場合は使ってくださいね	There is also a bathroom on the second floor. If the first-floor bathroom is crowded, please use it.
トイレの電気のスイッチはここです	The light switch for the toilet is here.

入浴

自衛隊が、仮設の入浴設備を設置してくれました	The temporary bathing facilities were installed by the Japan Self-Defense Force.
避難所から出ているバスで、入浴施設に行くことができます	There is a bus departing from the shelter that can take you to the bathing facilities.
入浴の際に介助が必要な方はおっしゃってください	If you need assistance when bathing, please let us know.
今お湯を沸かしています。もうしばらくお待ちください	We are currently heating the water. Please wait a little longer.
シャワーの代わりに足湯があります	There is a footbath instead of a shower.

▶寝具

支援物資として、毛布が送られてきたので、寝るときに使ってください	Relief blankets have been sent in, so please use them when you sleep.
毛布をもう1枚使いますか？	Would you like one more blanket?
夜は冷え込むので、もっと厚着をしたほうがいいかもしれません	It gets cold at night, so it's best to wear warmer clothing.
枕は1つでいい？	Is one pillow enough?
布団の湿気やカビが気になるなら、天日干ししてください	If you are worried about moisture and mold on your futon, hang it out in the sun.

▶炊き出し

有名なカレーチェーン店のCome Come Curryが、ABC公園で炊き出しをしています	A famous curry chain restaurant called Come Come Curry is serving food at ABC Park.
兵庫県から来たボランティアが、ラーメンをふるまってくれます	Volunteers from Hyogo Prefecture will treat us to ramen.
11時から、ボランティアによる炊き出しがあります	Volunteers will be serving food from 11 o'clock.
仮設住宅の高齢者を対象に、地元の自治会が定期的に炊き出しをしてくれます	The neighborhood council will be serving meals periodically for the elderly living in temporary housing.

ゴミの処理

燃えるゴミは避難所の裏庭にある焼却炉で燃やします	Burnable garbage is burned in the incinerator located behind the shelter.
ゴミ集積所はこの建物の裏です	The trash collection site is located behind this building.
ゴミ袋は足りていますか？	Do you have enough trash bags?
古新聞は捨てずに、掃除などに活用しましょう	Instead of throwing out old newspapers, use them for cleaning and other things.
ペットボトルにお湯を入れると、湯たんぽとして再利用できます	You can fill plastic bottles with hot water to re-use them as hot water bottles.

洗濯

水不足のため、みなさんそこの川で洗濯していますよ ☑ 東日本大震災のとき、実際に沢などで洗濯をされていたケースがあるそうです。	Due to a lack of water, everyone is doing laundry in the nearby river.
隣町に誰でも自由に使える「洗濯所」があります	There is a laundromat in the next town that anyone can use freely.
校庭の東側に洗濯物を干せるロープが張ってあります	There is a rope for hanging laundry on the east side of the schoolyard.
衣類をギザギザの部分に押し付けて洗うんですよ ☑ 「洗濯板」の使い方を説明しています。	You wash your clothes by rubbing them on the rungs.
こちらのハンガーや洗濯バサミは、自由に使ってください	Feel free to use these hangers and clothespins.

▶ペット

残念ですがここでは飼えないので、ペットホテルや動物病院に相談してもらえますか？	Unfortunately, you can't have pets here, so could you please consult with a pet hotel or an animal hospital?
山中小学校に、保護された動物が集められています	Rescued animals are being kept at Yamanaka Elementary School.
義援品のペットフードを希望者にお配りします	We will distribute donated pet food to those who need it.
避難所での生活中、ペットの世話をしてくれるボランティアの方がいます	Volunteers are available to take care of your pets while you are living in the evacuation shelter.

▶喫煙

校舎の裏に、喫煙所があります	The smoking area is behind the school building.
一緒に一服しませんか？	Do you want to go smoke together?
一本いただけますか？	Can I have a cigarette?
ライターをお貸ししましょうか？	Do you need a lighter?
喫煙は体に悪いですよ	Smoking is bad for your health.

飲みすぎないほうがいいですよ	You shouldn't drink too much.
義援品に発泡酒がありました。欲しい方はおっしゃってください	There was some low-malt beer in the donations. Let us know if you'd like some.
これはジュースではなくお酒ですよ	This isn't a soft drink; it's alcohol.
寝つきが悪いからといって、お酒によるのはよくありませんよ。睡眠の質が悪くなるんです	It's not good to drink alcohol just because you have trouble sleeping. It'll make your quality of sleep even worse.
ウイスキーはいかがですか？	Would you like some whisky?

明日は嵐になるようですよ	A storm will come tomorrow.
明日は３日ぶりに晴れそうですよ	It will be sunny tomorrow for the first time in three days.
明日は花粉の飛ぶ量が多くなるようですよ	The pollen count will be high tomorrow.
来週には梅雨入りしそうですよ	It looks like the rainy season is going to start next week.
明日は暑くてじめじめした１日になりそうですよ	It looks like tomorrow is going to be hot and humid all day.

避難所での生活と被災後の生活

サイズが小さすぎるようなら、XL を着てみますか？	If the size is too small, would you like to try an extra large?
やっと十分な数の毛布が届きました	We finally received enough blankets.
女性用の冬服が、たくさん届きました	We received a lot of women's winter clothes.
今日の午後、また救援物資が届く予定です	More relief supplies are scheduled to arrive this afternoon.
物資のリクエストは、何かありますか？	Are there any goods you would like to make a request for?

▶仮設住宅

原則として、仮設住宅には入居日から１年間、滞在できます	As a general rule, you can stay at the temporary house for a year after moving in.
３歳未満の乳幼児や、75歳以上の高齢者がいる世帯は、優先的に入居できます	Families with infants under three or elderly people over 75 have priority when moving in.
家賃と駐車場料金は無料です	Rent and parking are free.
光熱水費、共益費は入居世帯の負担とします	All utility and facility costs are the responsibility of the families
電話やファックス、メールで申し込めます。助けが必要なら、おっしゃってください	You can apply by phone, fax or mail. If you need assistance, let us know.

マスクをすると、風邪などの感染症予防になるんです	Wearing a mask can prevent you from infectious diseases such as cold.
頭痛薬は救護室にあります	Headache medicine is available in the first aid room.
救護室で、絆創膏をもらえますよ	You can get Band-Aids from the first-aid room.
血圧が気になる人のために血圧計を用意しています	For people worried about high blood pressure, we have a blood pressure meter.
ずっと同じ姿勢でいるとエコノミークラス症候群になることがあります。ときどき運動するといいですよ	If you stay in the same position for too long, you could get economy class syndrome. It's a good idea to move around every now and then.
しっかり水分補給をして、脱水症状を予防しましょう	Prevent dehydration by drinking plenty of fluids.
食中毒を防ぐため配られた食事はできるだけ早く召しあがってください	To prevent food poisoning, please eat the food you are given as soon as possible.
ただの風邪ではなさそうなので、病院に行きましょう	It might be more than just a cold, so let's go to the hospital.
後日、医者が診察に来るので、不安なことがあったら相談するといいですよ	A doctor is coming the day after tomorrow to do medical examinations, so you should talk to them if you have any concerns.
英語が話せる心理カウンセラーがいるそうなので、話してみたらどうですか？	I hear they have a psychologist who can speak English. Why don't you try talking to them?

困ったことがあれば、いつでも私に相談してください	Please come to me anytime when you are in trouble.
それを運ぶのをお手伝いしますよ	I'll help you carry that.
あなたへの伝言を預かっています	I have a message for you.
衛星電話を無料で使うことができますよ	You can use a satellite phone for free.
非常時なので、公衆電話は無料で使うことができます	Since we're in a state of emergency, public phones can be used free of charge.
これは使い捨てカイロです。袋から取り出して振ると、すぐに温かくなります	This is a disposable heating pad. Take it out of the package, shake it and it will warm up quickly.
これは「蚊取り線香」といって、煙で蚊を追い払います	This is a "mosquito coil." The smoke repels mosquitos.
蚊がたくさんいるので、この虫よけを使ってください	There are lots of mosquitos, so use this insect repellent.
みんなで一緒に運動しませんか？	Would you like to come exercise with everyone now?
今後、震度5くらいの余震が発生することも十分考えられるそうです	From here on, we can expect aftershocks of around level 5 intensity to take place.

情報を提供する・アドバイスする（女性）

女性特有の悩みに対して配慮する

生理用品は足りていますか？	Do you have enough sanitary supplies?
生理痛なら、薬をさしあげましょうか？	If you have menstrual cramps, would you like some medicine?
冷え症なら、この使い捨てカイロを使ってください	If you are sensitive to the cold, please use this disposable heating pad.
このトイレは女性専用です	This restroom is for women only.
下着はこちらのパーティションの中に干せますよ	You can hang underwear within this partition.

化粧や服装などに配慮する

水のいらないシャンプーを配っています。使いますか？	We are distributing dry shampoo. Would you like some?
こちらの部屋に簡単な化粧台を用意してあります	You can find a simple vanity table in this room.
化粧水と乳液が寄付されたので、みなさんで分け合ってください	Face lotion and cream have been donated, so please share.
こちらのコットンは、ご自由にお使いください	Please help yourself to this cotton.
配給された衣服はサイズ別に分けてありますので、1人3着ずつ持って行ってください	Clothing rations are separated by size. Please take three sets per person.

この電気ポットのお湯は、調乳用に使って構いません	You may use the hot water from the hot pot for baby formula. ☑ baby formula「粉ミルク」
授乳の際は、この部屋をお使いください。カギをかけられます	Please use this room when breastfeeding. The door locks.
授乳用ケープがございます。必要な方はおっしゃってください	Nursing covers are available. Please let us know if you need to use one.
哺乳瓶を貸し出しています。1人3本までです	We are lending out three baby bottles per person.
必要な方に赤ちゃん用の洗濯洗剤を提供しています	We will provide baby-friendly laundry detergent when needed.
紙おむつは足りていますか？	Do you have enough disposable diapers?
赤ちゃん用おしりふきや綿棒が必要でしたら、おっしゃってくださいね	If you need any baby wipes or cotton swabs, please let us know.
離乳食を希望者に配布しております	We are distributing baby food to those who need it.
古着のベビー服が届きましたので、自由にご覧ください	We have received some used baby clothes. You're free to look through them.
こちらの粉ミルク缶は、ご自由にお使いください	Help yourself to the cans of powdered baby formula.

生活習慣や宗教の違いに配慮する

トイレ

和式トイレの使い方はわかりますか？	Do you know how to use Japanese-style toilets?
このトイレは和式で、しゃがんで用を足します	This is a Japanese-style toilet that is used by squatting.
洋式のトイレはこちらにあります	Western-style toilets are located here.
すみません、ここには和式トイレしかないんです	Sorry, there are only Japanese-style toilets here.
この出っ張り部分は便座ではありません。しゃがむ方向を間違えないように	This part sticking out here is not a toilet seat. Be sure to face in the right direction when squatting.

寝具

これは「敷布団」なので、広げて、その上に寝てください	This is a futon mattress, so please lay it out and sleep on top of it.
これは掛け布団カバーです	This is a cover for the bed comforter.
ベッドはないので、床に布団を敷いてください	There are no beds, so please lay out futons on the floor.
布団はたためばコンパクトになって、場所を取りませんよ	If you fold your futon and make it compact, it won't take up space.

▶ 入浴習慣

日本には、シャワーだけでなく、浴槽でお湯につかる習慣があります	Besides showering, there is also a custom of soaking in a hot bath in Japan.
日本では公衆浴場が一般的です。ときには大勢の人が一度に入浴することもあります	Public bathing is common in Japan. There may be many people bathing at once.
共同風呂に入る前には、軽く体を流すのがマナーです	Rinsing off before entering the public bath shows consideration for others.
体の泡をしっかり落としてから浴槽に入ってください	Please rinse all soap from your body before entering the bath.
バスタブの中で、体を洗わないでください	Please do not wash your body inside the bathtub.

▶ 文化的・宗教的習慣

周りの迷惑になるので、お香を焚かないでください	To avoid disturbing those around you, please do not burn incense.
お祈りをするときは、3年2組の教室を使っていただけますか？	For prayer, could you please use classroom 3-2?
香辛料などの、臭いのきついものを出しっぱなしにしないでください	Please do not leave spices or other odorous materials sitting out.
隣町に、ABC教会という教会がありますよ	There is a church called ABC Church in the next town.
近くにモスクがあるかどうか調べましょうか？	Would you like me to see if there is a mosque nearby?

▶ 避難者の家族構成など

お一人ですか？	Are you by yourself?
ご家族の方はご一緒ですか？	Is your family with you?
世帯ごとにこの書類を記入してください。不明点があれば、運営委員の誰かに聞いてくださいね	Please fill out this form as a family. If there's anything you don't understand, please ask one of the staff.
行方がわからないご家族のお名前、性別、年齢、所属をこの用紙にご記入ください	Please write the name, sex, age and school or workplace of any family member(s) whose whereabouts are unknown using this form.
携帯番号がわかれば、それも用紙に記入してください	If you know the person's mobile phone number, please include it in the form.
ご家族とは連絡が取れていますか？	Are you able to contact your family?
お母様とはどこではぐれたのですか？	Where did you get separated from your mother?
地震が発生した時間は、息子さんは小学校にいたはずですよね？	Your son was supposed to be at the elementary school when the earthquake happened, right?
連絡の取れているご家族はいますか？	Are there any family members that you are keeping in contact with?
お父さんの勤め先はわかる？	Do you know your dad's workplace?

▶ 健康状態など

体調はいかがですか？	How are you feeling?
疲れていませんか？	Are you tired?
どこか痛みますか？	Do you have any pain anywhere?
腰痛の具合はいかがですか？	How is your back pain?
食欲はありますか？	Do you have an appetite?
食事はちゃんと食べられていますか？	Are you eating properly?
排泄は普段通りにできていますか？	Are you able to go to the bathroom normally?
持病がおありと聞いておりますが、具合はいかがですか？	I heard you have a chronic condition. How are you feeling?
お薬はちゃんと飲まれていますか？	Are you properly taking your medicine?
薬は足りていますか？	Do you have enough medicine?
熱はありますか？	Do you have a fever?
のどは痛くありませんか？	Do you have a sore throat?

夜はちゃんと眠れていますか？	Are you getting enough sleep at night?
寝つきはいいですか？	Are you able to sleep okay?
歩けますか？	Are you able to walk?
階段の上り下りはできますか？	Can you go up and down stairs?
歩くのに杖が必要ですか？	Do you need a cane to walk?
車イスが必要ですか？	Do you need a wheelchair?
入れ歯や差し歯をお使いですか？	Do you use dentures or have teeth implants?
虫歯はありますか？	Do you have any cavities?
めまいや立ちくらみはありませんか？	Do you feel any dizziness or vertigo?
この2週間で体重に変化はありましたか？	Have there been any changes in your body weight in the past two weeks?
気持ちが落ち込み、気力がない状態が続いていますか？	Do you still feel depressed and out of energy?

▶ 食べ物

何か食べらないものはありますか？	Are there any foods that you cannot eat?
もっと軟らかく調理したほうがよろしいですか？	Would it be better to cook it softer?
アレルギーのある食べ物はありますか？	Do you have any food allergies?
あなたはベジタリアンですか？	Are you a vegetarian?
魚や貝類は食べられますか？	Can you eat fish and shellfish?

▶ 衣類

サイズを教えてください	What size are you?
ご家族一人ひとりの服と靴のサイズをこの用紙にご記入ください	Please fill in each family member's clothing and shoe sizes in the form.
どのような衣類が必要ですか？	What kind of clothing do you need?
下着は足りていますか？	Do you have enough underwear?
息子さんの身長は何センチですか？	How tall is your son in centimeters?
冬の上着はお持ちですか？	Do you have a winter coat?

お家の被害状況はどのようなものですか？	How badly was your home damaged?
家で何か壊れたものはありますか？	Is there anything broken at your home?
外壁や塀は損壊しませんでしたか？	Have any exterior walls or fences been damaged?
お家は津波の被害に遭われましたか？	Did the tsunami cause any damage to your home?
家から持ち出す必要があるものはありますか？	Are there any belongings that need to be taken from your home?
家の被害状況を、全壊・半壊・一部損壊から選んでください	Please rate the level of damage to your home as full, half or partial.
ご自宅は浸水していますか？	Is your home flooded?
窓ガラスなどは割れましたか？	Were the windows or anything else broken or damaged?
自動車はお持ちですか？ その自動車は無事ですか？	Do you own a car? If so, was it damaged?
火災の被害はありましたか？	Was there any damage from the fire?
家は傾いていますか？	Is your house tilted?

▶ 仮設住宅

仮設住宅への入居を希望しますか？	Would you like to move into temporary housing?
大人何名、子ども何名ですか？	How many adults and children?
仮設住宅を希望しますか、それとも民間の賃貸アパートがよいですか？	Would you like to move into temporary housing or a rented apartment?
部屋数を1、2、3部屋から選べます	You can choose one, two or three rooms.
手すりやスロープがある部屋のほうがいいですか？	Would you prefer an apartment with handles and ramps?

▶ その他の確認事項

粉ミルクは必要ですか？	Do you need baby formula?
布団や毛布は足りていますか？	Do you have enough futons and blankets?
通帳と印鑑はお持ちですか？	Do you have your account book and personal seal with you?
ご自宅は、ちゃんと施錠されましたか？	Is your home properly locked?
あなたの家は持家ですか、それとも借家ですか？	Do you own or rent your house?

全般

何か足りないものはありますか？	Is there anything that you're short on?
何か困っていることはありませんか？	Are you having any trouble with anything?
何か心配事はありませんか？	Do you have any concerns about anything?
自国のご家族と連絡は取れましたか？	Were you able to contact your family in your country?
余震に注意してください	Please be careful of aftershocks.
暖かくして、ゆっくりやすんでくださいね	Please stay warm and get plenty of rest.
こまめにうがい・手洗いをして、風邪をひかないようこしてくださいね	Gargle and wash your hands frequently and take care not to catch a cold.
乾燥しているので、火の元には注意しましょう	Please be careful not to cause fires because the air is dry.
助け合って、この困難を乗り切りましょう	Let's help each other get through this difficult time.
この避難所の生活に慣れましたか？	Have you gotten used to living in this evacuation center?

避難所での生活と被災後の生活

▶お年寄り

自宅から取ってくるものがあれば、私も同行してお手伝いします	If there is anything you need to get from your home, I'll come along and help you.
重そうですね。私が運びましょうか？	That looks heavy. Shall I carry it for you?
私が支えますので、ゆっくり上りましょう	I'll support you. Let's go up slowly.
薄い味付けの食事がいいですか？	Is it better for you to eat bland foods?
一緒に、お散歩に行きませんか？	Would you like to go for a walk together?

▶子ども

大丈夫だから、心配しないでね	It's okay, don't worry.
しばらくの間、頑張ろうね	We have to hang in there for a while.
近いうちに、きっと家に戻れるからね	I'm sure you'll be back home soon.
きっとまた学校に通える日が来るよ	I'm sure you'll go back to school again someday.
元気がないみたいだけど、どうかした？	You don't look happy, what's wrong?
お母さんは、きっと無事だよ	I'm sure your mom is okay.

特別永住者証明書の提示を求めています	They are asking for your special permanent resident certificate.
パスポートを見せてほしいそうです	They want you to show your passport.
在留カード（外国人登録証）を見せてほしいそうです	They want you to show your residence card.
用紙に、家族構成を記入してほしいそうです	They want you to fill in your immediate family members' information on this form.
この書類に不明な点があったら、おっしゃってください	If there is anything you don't understand on this document, please let us know.
住民票を見せてください。「住民票」には自分の住所を証明するものです	Please show your certificate of residence. It is used to verify your address.
国民健康保険に加入していますか？	Do you have national health insurance?
通っている学校名を教えてください	Please tell me the name of the school you attend.
あの日にお子さんが着ていた服を説明してください	Please describe the clothes your child was wearing that day.
友人のジョシュア・ニールさんの居場所を知っていますか？	Do you know the whereabouts of your friend, Joshua Neal?

避難所での生活と被災後の生活

外国人ボランティアの受け入れ

▶注意事項・ルールの説明

必ず防塵マスク、厚手で長めのゴム手袋、長靴を着用してください	You must wear a dust mask, long thick rubber gloves and boots.
もしできない作業があれば、言ってくださいね	If there is a job you can't do, please tell us.
多くの作業は協力が必要です。コミュニケーションを取り、気をつけながら共に働きましょう	Most jobs require the cooperation of others. Communicate, work together and use caution.
自分のゴミは持ち帰ってください	Take your trash home with you.
必ずボランティア保険に加入してください	You must register for volunteer's insurance.
天候によっては、作業内容が変わることがあります	The job details could change with the weather.
何かを捨てる際には、必ず家主に確認してください	Please confirm with the home owner before throwing anything away.
休憩は自己判断で適宜取ってください	Use your own judgment in deciding appropriate break times.
このタンスはとても重いですよ	This chest is very heavy.
ケガしないよう、十分気をつけて作業してくださいね	Please do your work carefully to avoid injury.

物資の荷卸しを手伝ってもらえませんか？	Could you help unload supplies?
物資を保管場所へ運ぶのを手伝ってもらえませんか？	Could you help move these supplies to the storage area?
これらの洋服を女性用と男性用に分けてもらえますか？	Can you separate these clothes into men's and women's?
そのまな板を使って食材を切ってもらえますか？	Can you cut the food on that cutting board?
彼のしているように、これらのゴミの袋をトラックに積み込んでもらえますか？	Can you load these trash bags into the truck like he's doing?
隣町で瓦礫の撤去作業を手伝ってもらえませんか？	Could you help remove debris in the next town?
今日は、路上の瓦礫除去の手伝いをお願いします	Today, please help clear debris from the street.
泥はこの土嚢に入れてください	Please put mud in these sandbags.
ここに穴を掘ってもらえますか？	Can you dig a hole here, please?
線路の復旧作業を手伝ってください	Please help repair the train tracks.

避難所での生活と被災後の生活

貴重品や思い出の品と思われるものは、この箱に入れてください	Put things that can be considered valuable or memorabilia in this box.
この薪を割ってください	Please cut this firewood.
仮設住宅から荷物を運び出すのを手伝ってください	Please help carry things out of the temporary housing.
倒木の撤去作業を手伝ってもらえませんか？	Can you help remove fallen trees?
その作業が終わったら、声をかけてもらえますか？	Could you tell me when you finish that job?

▶ お礼を言う

遠路はるばるお越しいただき、本当にありがとうございます	Thank you very much for coming all the way out here.
お疲れさまでした。明日もよろしくお願いします	Thanks for everything today. See you tomorrow.
復興には長い時間がかかります。ご協力お願いします	Reconstruction takes a long time. We ask for your cooperation.
日本全体を代表して、お礼を申し上げます	Thank you on behalf of all of Japan.
あなたの国で大きな災害があったときは、必ず駆けつけますね	We will go right away to help you when there is a big disaster in your country.

非常時のアナウンス

余震発生時

ただ今、震度4の地震が発生しました	There has just been an intensity 4 earthquake.
マグニチュードは5.2。震源は茨城県沖です	The magnitude was 5.2. The epicenter was off the coast of Ibaraki Prefecture.
この地震による津波の心配はありません	This earthquake does not pose a tsunami threat.
この地域に津波警報が出ています	A tsunami warning has been issued for this area.
安全のため、直ちに避難してください	Please evacuate immediately to safety.

津波について

津波の到達予想時刻は午後4時40分。予想の高さは1メートルです	The expected tsunami arrival time is 4:40 pm. The expected height is one meter.
到達時刻はあくまでも目安です	This is an estimated time of arrival.
津波は、予想よりも高くなることがあります	The tsunami could be higher than expected.
津波が内陸深くまで流れ込む可能性があります	There is a possibility the tsunami run-up could continue far inland.
津波は何度も押し寄せ、急に高くなることもあります	Tsunamis could keep coming, causing water levels to rise quickly.

避難所での生活と被災後の生活

Chapter 5

その他の災害および事故・事件

雷

▶ 雷の予報を伝える

予報によれば、雷を伴う激しい夕立になるそうです	The forecast calls for thunderstorms.
雷注意報が発令されています。外に出ないでください	A lightning advisory has been issued. Please stay inside.
明日、関東地方は激しい雷雨に見舞われるようです	The Kanto region will have thunderstorms tomorrow.
雷雨は明日の朝まで続くそうですよ	The thunderstorm will last until tomorrow morning.

▶ 雷の状況を伝える

外は激しい雷雨です	There's heavy rain and thunder outside.
まだ（雷は）遠いよ	The lightning is still far from here
光と雷鳴の間隔が近くなっているので、雷は近づいています	The time between the lightning and thunder is shorter, so it must be getting closer.
雷雲は西から東へはやい速度で移動しています	Thunder clouds are moving from west to east at high speeds.
この辺りでは、深夜1時ごろに雷雨がピークを迎えるようです	The thunderstorm will reach its climax around 1:00 in the morning in this area.
あそこの木に雷が落ちました	That tree was just struck by lightning.

あの建物の中に避難しましょう	Let's seek shelter inside that building.
木のそばには行かないように	Do not go near any trees.
自動車の中は比較的安全です	You are relatively safe inside motor vehicles.
傘はささないほうがいいですよ	You should not use an umbrella.
両足を揃えてしゃがんで、目を閉じ、指で両耳穴をふさいでください	Crouch down with your legs together, close your eyes and put your fingers in your ears.
電話線をすべて、差し込み口から抜いてください	Unplug all phone cords from their sockets.
このマンションには避雷針がついていますから、安心してください	Don't worry. This apartment building has a lightning rod.
開けたところにいるのは危険ですよ	Staying in open spaces is dangerous.
金属を身に付けていなくても、雷に打たれる危険は十分にあるんですよ	Even if you don't have anything metallic on your body, there is still a good chance of being struck by lightning.
落雷によって火災が発生するケースもあるんですよ	A lightning strike can cause a fire.

その他の災害および事故・事件

▶降雪の予報や状況を伝える

今週末、関東地方は大雪になるそうですよ	The Kanto region will get heavy snow this weekend.
甲府市では、明日朝までの積雪が50センチを超えると予想されています	The accumulated snowfall in Kofu is expected to surpass 50 centimeters by tomorrow morning.
明日は1日中雪が降り続くそうです	They're saying it will snow all day tomorrow.
横殴りの激しい雪が降っています	Heavy snow is blowing sideways.
雪と風がひどく、1メートル先が見えないほどです	There's so much snow and wind that it's difficult to see one meter ahead of you.

▶雪害に対して注意を呼びかける

猛吹雪だから、家から出ないようにしてください	There's a violent snowstorm, so please stay inside.
雪崩に注意してください	Watch out for avalanches. ☑ avalanche はアバランチと発音します。
落雪に注意してください	Be careful of snow falling from high places.
道路や歩道の一部が凍っているので、滑って転ばないように注意してください	Some parts of the road and sidewalks are icy, so be careful not to slip or fall.
そんな滑りやすい靴で外を歩くと、転びますよ	If you go outside with such slippery shoes, you're likely to slip and fall.

スタッドレスタイヤじゃないと、運転するのは危険だよ	Driving on anything other than winter tires is dangerous.
雪道では徐行運転をするように	Be sure to drive slowly on snow.
雪やつららが屋根から落ちてくるかもしれないので、注意してください	Snow or icicles may fall from the roof, so be careful. ☑ icicle はアイスィクルと発音します。
屋根の雪下ろしをしないと、家がつぶれてしまいますよ	If we don't clear the snow off the roof, it could cave in.
建物から離れたところに駐車・駐輪をしたほうが安全ですよ	It's safer to park your car or bike away from buildings.

交通機関などへの影響に対して注意を呼びかける

雪の影響で、列車が大幅に遅れています	Due to the snow, trains are severely delayed.
JR線の一部の列車は運転を見合わせています。	Some trains on the JR lines have been temporarily stopped.
除雪作業が終わるまで、列車は動きそうもありませんよ	Until all the snow has been cleared off, the trains will not be running.
大雪のため、高速道路は全面通行止めです	Due to heavy snowfall, traffic on all highways has been stopped.
飛行機は欠航が多くなっているようなので、出発する前に確認したほうがいいですよ	It looks like many flights have been canceled, so check before leaving.

その他の災害および事故・事件

雹（ひょう）

▶降雹の予報や状況を伝える

今夜は雪ではなく雹が降るかもしれないそうですよ	They're saying that instead of snow, hail may fall tonight.
一時的に雹が降りそうです	Hail is expected to fall for a short time.
外では1センチの大きさの雹が降っていますよ	There's one-centimeter hail falling outside.
現在、西東京市では雹が降り、風も強く吹いています	Currently, there are hail and strong winds in Nishi-Tokyo City.
雹が激しく屋根に当たる音です	It sounds like hail is falling really hard on the roof.

▶注意を呼びかける

ゴルフボール大の雹が降っているので、外に出ないでください	Golf ball-sized hail is falling outside, so please stay inside.
雹が降ってきたら、すぐ屋内に入るように	If it begins to hail, get inside as soon as possible.
たとえ小さくても、速度がついた雹は破壊を引き起こします	Even small hail can cause damage when falling at high speeds.
雹でケガをする場合もあるので、気をつけてください	You can get injured by hail, so please be careful.
雹で車がへこむかもしれません	Hail can dent cars.

猛暑

猛暑の予報や状況を伝える

ものすごい暑さなので、外に出ないほうがいいですよ	It's very hot outside, so it's best to stay indoors.
今日の最高気温は37度になるそうです	It looks like today's high temperature will be 37 degrees.
明日もこの暑さなら、7日連続の猛暑日となります	If this heat continues tomorrow, it will be seven days of extremely hot weather.
熱中症になる人が続出しているそうですよ	It seems that there are a lot of people suffering from heatstroke.
この猛暑で、多くのお年寄りが亡くなられたそうですよ	It seems that a lot of elderly people have died due to the extreme heat.

暑さへの対策をアドバイスする

水分をたくさん取ってください	Be sure to drink plenty of fluids.
この暑さでは、エアコンをつけないと、室内にいても熱中症になってしまいますよ	In this heat, if you don't turn on the air conditioner, you can get heatstroke while indoors.
帽子をかぶったほうがいいですよ	It's best to wear a hat.
水分と同時に塩分を補給することも重要です	Along with fluids, be sure to replenish the minerals in your body as well.

アスファルトがとても熱くなっているので、小さい子どもの体調に気をつけてください	The asphalt has become very hot, so be mindful of small children's conditions. ☑ 小さい子どもはより地表熱の影響を受けやすいため。
乳幼児は体温調節がうまくできないので、熱中症になりやすいんですよ	Infants can't control their temperature well, so there is danger of heatstroke.
子どもを車内に置き去りにしないでくださいね	Please do not leave your children locked inside your car.
用心するに越したことはないので、日焼け止めを塗ってください	It's better to be safe than sorry, so put on some sunscreen.

▶ 体調を崩したときの対処法を教える

エアコンの効いている部屋に移動しましょう	Please move to a properly air-conditioned room.
シャツのボタンをゆるめて、日陰で横になってください	Loosen up your shirt buttons and lie down in the shade.
彼／彼女にスポーツドリンクを飲ませてください	Give him/her some sports drink.
濡れタオルを持ってきてください。彼／彼女の首すじや脇の下を冷やします	Bring me a wet towel. I'm going to cool his/her neck and underarms.
めまいや頭痛を訴える人がいたら、足を高くして寝かせてください	If anyone is suffering from dizziness or a headache, have them lie down with their legs up.

竜巻の予報や状況を伝える

竜巻などの突風は予測が難しいので、突然襲ってくるケースがほとんどです	It's very difficult to predict a tornado strike, as they tend to appear suddenly.
滋賀県に竜巻注意報が発表されました。念のため注意してください	A tornado advisory has been issued in Shiga Prefecture. Be careful just in case.
竜巻が見えるぞ！	I can see the tornado!
近くで竜巻が発生したそうですよ	A tornado has been spotted nearby.
外はものすごい突風が吹いています	It's extremely windy outside.

注意を呼びかける

竜巻が過ぎ去るまで絶対に外に出ないでください	Do not go outside until the tornado passes.
今すぐ頑丈な建物の中に避難しましょう	Take refuge in a sturdy building right away.
シャッターを閉めてください	Please close the shutters.
外にいると危険なので、あのビルの中に入りましょう	It's dangerous to stay outside, so let's go inside that building.
飛来物に十分気をつけてください	Watch out for flying objects.

噴火

▶噴火の予報や状況を伝える

富士山が噴火するかもしれないというニュースがありました	The news said Mt. Fuji could erupt.
阿蘇山に噴火警報が発令されました	A volcanic eruption warning has been issued for Mt. Aso.
警戒レベルは3なので、入山規制がされています。念のため避難の準備をしてください	The current security level is 3, so access to the mountain is restricted. Prepare for an evacuation just in case.
この山も活火山ですよ	This mountain is also an active volcano.
大地震の後には、噴火が起こる可能性が高くなるそうです	It seems that, after a large earthquake, the chances of an eruption increase.

▶注意を呼びかける

火砕流に巻き込まれたら生き延びることはできません。今すぐ避難しましょう	If we get caught in the pyroclastic flow, we won't survive. We need to run now. ☑ pyroclastic はパイロクラスティックと発音します。
大きな噴石は屋根を打ち破ることもあります	Large volcanic rocks can smash the roofs of houses.
この地域にもうすぐ火山灰が降ってくると予想されています	They predict that volcanic ash will start coming down soon in this area.
有毒な火山ガスが発生しているので、火口から離れてください	Poisonous gases are being expelled by the volcano, so please stay away from its crater.

停電の可能性を知らせる（準備させる）

台風の影響で、停電になるかもしれません	The typhoon may cause blackouts.
停電に備えて、懐中電灯を用意しておいてください	Keep a flashlight handy in case of a blackout.
今日の午後2時から午後8時まで、この地区は計画停電になるそうです	A scheduled power outage will take place today in this region from 2:00 to 8:00 pm.
急な停電に備えて、冷蔵庫はなるべく閉めっぱなしにしておいてください ☑中の食料品が傷むのを防ぐため。	Try to keep your refrigerator door closed in case of a sudden blackout.

停電に対処する

懐中電灯やろうそくはありますか？	Do you have a flashlight or candles?
空調が止まってしまったので、窓を開けましょう	The ventilation isn't working, so please open the window.
エアコンは使えませんが石油ストーブなら使えます	You can't use the air conditioner, but you can use an oil heater.
ブレーカーはどこにありますか？	Where's your fuse box?
ブレーカーを「入」に戻してください	Please return the breaker switch to the "on" position.

隣のビルも停電していますか？	Is the power out in the building next door as well?
停電は、この部屋だけですか？ それとも、建物全体ですか？	Is your apartment the only one experiencing a power failure or is it the entire building?
懐中電灯をとってきますね	I'll go get a flashlight.
電力会社に電話してみます	I'll try calling the electric company.
漏電しているかもしれないので、注意してください	There may be a short circuit so please be careful.

▶ 停電になったときの声かけ

しばらくしたら回復すると思いますよ	It should come back on soon.
暗闇でむやみに歩くとケガをしますよ	You'll hurt yourself walking in the dark.
そのうち目が慣れて、見えるようになりますよ	Once your eyes get used to it, you'll be able to see.
慌てないで！ その場で動かずじっとしていてください	Don't panic! Just stay there.
自家発電に自動で切り変わるはずですよ	The in-house backup generator should come on automatically.

断水

断水になったことを知らせる

断水しています	The water has been cut off.
水が出ないので、断水かもしれません	The water's not coming out, so it must have been cut off.
断水なので、トイレの水は流せません	The water's out, so you can't flush the toilet.
水道管を交換する工事が行われるので、4時まで断水になります	They'll be changing the pipes, so the water will be off until 4:00.

その他

復旧時に備えて、蛇口は必ず閉めてください	Be sure to turn off the faucets before the water comes back on.
断水に備えて浴槽に水をためておくと便利ですよ	It's a good idea to keep your tub full of water in case the water goes out.
給水車が巡回して、水を配給してくれるそうです	The water tank truck will be going around and distributing water.
飲み水はありますか? なければお分けしますので、おっしゃってくださいね	Do you have drinkable water? If not, I can share some with you, so let me know.
水が透明になるまで、しばらく出しっぱなしにしておきましょう	Keep the tap running until the water runs clear.

交通事故

▶ 事故現場で

前の交差点で、交通事故が起きたようです	It looks like there was an accident at the intersection ahead.
三角停止表示板か発煙筒を置いて、後続車に知らせなくては	We have to set a warning triangle or emergency flare to notify cars coming up behind us.
そこの角で車に人がはねられたようなんですが、事故の瞬間を見ましたか？	It seems like someone was run over by a car on that corner. Were you watching when it happened?
はねられた人はお知り合いですか？	Do you know the person who got hit?
ひき逃げだ！ 車のナンバーをメモして！	It's a hit-and-run! Write down the license plate number!

▶ 被害者を救助する

どこか痛みますか？	Does it hurt anywhere?
救急車を呼びますか？	Should we call an ambulance?
私は AED を探してきます	I'll look for the AED.
後続事故の恐れがあるので、歩道に移動しましょう	There could be another accident so let's move onto the sidewalk.
はねられた人は頭を負傷しているので、むやみに動かさないでください	The person hit by a car has a head injury, so don't let them move too much.

列車事故

事故現場に居合わせた場合

危ないから押さないでください	It's dangerous, so please don't push.
ケガをした人はいませんか？	Is anybody injured?
生存者の救助を手伝ってください	Please help me with assisting the survivors.
後続列車が来ているかもしれないので、非常停止ボタンを押してください	The next train may come, so please press the emergency stop button.
線路に降りるのは危険です。係員の指示を待ちましょう	Stepping down onto the tracks is dangerous. Let's wait for instructions from the staff.

その他

人身事故のため、電車はすべて止まっています	Due to an accident with injuries, all trains are stopped.
故障のため、この電車は止まっています	The train is stopped due to a malfunction.
鶯谷駅と上野駅の間の民家で火災が発生したため、山手線の外回りは運転を見合わせています	Operation of the outer tracks of the Yamanote Line has been suspended due to house fires between Uguisudani and Ueno Stations.
最寄りの駅まで歩いて移動してください	Please walk to the nearest train station.
状況を確認してくるので、ここで待っていてください	Please wait here while I confirm the situation.

海難事故

▶乗っていた船が事故に遭った場合

本船は台風の影響で座礁しました	Due to the typhoon, our ship has been grounded.
本船は漁船と衝突しましたが、沈没の危険はないので、どうぞ落ち着いてください	This boat collided with a fishing boat, but there is no danger of sinking, so please remain calm.
現在、救助船がこちらに向かっているとの情報が入りました	We received information that the rescue ship is now on its way.
救命胴衣を直ちに着用してください	Please put on a life jacket immediately.
救命ボートに移ってください	Please get on the rescue boat.

▶救助活動

こちらの船に飛び乗ってください！	Please jump onto our boat!
海上保安庁に連絡したので、すぐに救助が来ますよ	I called the Coast Guard, so help should arrive soon.
担架か、その代わりになるものを持ってきてください	Please bring a stretcher or something to use as a stretcher.
このロープにつかまってください	Please hold on to this rope.

水難事故・山岳事故

川や海で

その辺りは潮の流れが速いので行かないでください	There's a really strong current there, so stay away.
波が高くなってきたぞ！ 海から上がって！	The waves are getting higher! Get off the beach!
ダムが放水を開始したぞ！ 増水するから、水から上がって！	The floodgates on the dam have been opened! Water levels will rise, so get out!
私の手につかまって。引き上げますよ	Grab my hand. I'll pull you up.
酔った状態で川に入らないでください	Please refrain from swimming in the river when drunk.

山で

落石だ！ 頭上に気をつけて！	Rocks are falling. Watch above you.
むやみに歩くのはやめよう。ここで助けが来るのを待とう	Don't wander off. Let's wait for help to arrive.
下山して、助けを呼んできてもらえますか？	Can you go down the mountain to get help?
そっちは崖だよ	There's a cliff there.
熊だ！ 走って逃げてはダメだよ。ゆっくり後ずさりして！	It's a bear! Don't run away. Step back slowly!

原発事故

▶原発事故の状況を伝える

大田原発が、メルトダウンしかかっているそうです	They're saying a meltdown is in progress at the Ota Nuclear Power Plant.
大田原発の2号機で、水素爆発が起こったそうです	It seems there was a hydrogen explosion at Ota Nuclear Power Plant reactor 2.
今もなお放射性物質が大気中に放出され続けています	Radioactive material is still being released into the atmosphere.
この事故は人的ミスで起きました	This accident was caused by human error.
格納容器の圧力を下げるため、1時間以内にベントが行われます	To release pressure within the containment vessel, ventilation will take place with an hour.

▶放射能汚染の情報を伝える

この地区の汚染レベルは、それほど甚大ではありません	The contamination level in this area is not that great.
山本小学校の校庭に、いくつかホットスポットがあるようです	It seems some hot spots have been detected on the grounds of Yamamoto Elementary School.
水道水の汚染濃度が高いので、飲まないでください	The tap water is highly contaminated, so please don't drink it.
放射能レベルが高いので、屋外に出ないでください	Please don't go outside because the radiation levels are high.

大田原発から半径20キロ圏内は、立ち入りが禁止されています	An area of 20 kilometers around the Ota Nuclear Power Plant has become a prohibited area.
この地域の住民には、避難命令が出されています	An evacuation order has been issued for people living in this area.
放射性物質に汚染されていないか一人一人検査されるそうです	They will test everyone for radioactive contamination.
危険なレベルの汚染濃度になっているので、直ちに避難してください	Contamination is reaching dangerous levels, so evacuate immediately.

その他

放射能測定器はネット通販で購入できますよ	You can buy a radiation detector online.
このスーパーの食品は、すべて放射線検査済みです	All food items from this supermarket have already been tested for radiation.
野菜は、よく洗えば、表面の放射性物質を除去できますよ	If you wash vegetables well, you can remove surface radiation.
この抗放射線薬を直ちに服用してください	Take this anti-radiation pill immediately.
うわさに惑わされないように	Try not to believe rumors.

その他の災害および事故・事件

テロ

▶ 発生したテロ事件の情報を伝える

東京駅で、爆弾テロが発生したというニュースが流れています	There's been a report of a terrorist bombing at Tokyo Station.
国会議事堂の前で自爆テロが発生したそうです	It seems there's been a suicide bombing in front of the Diet Building.
過激派グループが、人質をとって、ABC社の社長宅に立てこもっています	A group of extremists has taken several hostages and are in the ABC Company president's house
市庁舎に爆弾を仕掛けた、という電話がかかってきたそうです	It seems that someone phoned in a bomb threat at city hall.
お昼ごろ、横浜駅でナイフを持った男が近くにいた4人を次々と襲う事件があったそうです	It seems that, at Yokohama Station around noon, a man with a knife attacked four people standing near him.
連続爆破テロが発生しているので、十分に警戒してください	There have been a series of terrorist bombing attacks, so be careful.
ABC社の冷凍食品にヒ素を混入させたという声明が警察に届き、回収騒ぎになっています	There's been talk of a recall after someone sent a statement to the police saying he had mixed arsenic into ABC Company's frozen foods.
犯人はいまだ逃走中です	The culprit is still on the loose.
さくらカードの会員18万人分の個人情報が漏えいしたそうです	The personal information of 180,000 Sakura Card members has been leaked.

テロ現場に居合わせた場合

誰か警察に電話してください	Someone please call the police.
とにかく、ここから離れましょう。私についてきてください	In any event, let's get away from this place. Please follow me.
ガスを吸い込まないように、口にハンカチをあてて逃げましょう	While we escape, cover your mouth with a handkerchief, so you don't breath in gas.
大声を出すと犯人を刺激してしまうので、静かにしましょう	If you raise your voice, you'll alert the criminal, so let's be quiet.
犯行グループの要求に黙って従いましょう	We should do whatever criminal organizations tell us to.

その他

地下鉄で毒ガステロが発生したらしく、ほとんどの路線が運行を見合わせています	It seems that there's been a terror-related poisonous gas attack on the subway, and most of the lines have stopped.
山田さんの息子さんが、テロ事件に巻き込まれたそうです	It seems that Mr. Yamada's son has gotten caught up in some terrorist incident.
アメリカ大統領が訪問中なので、テロ対策として、主要道路で検問が行われています	The president of the United States is currently visiting, so in an effort to combat terror, they have put checkpoints on the main roads.
新宿駅で毒ガステロがあったようですが、君は今どこにいますか？	I heard there was a terror-related poisonous gas attack at Shinjuku Station. Where are you now?

その他の災害および事故・事件

テロ **165**

その他の災害

▶ハチに刺されたら

その現場からすぐ10メートル以上離れてください	Quickly get ten meters or more away from the area.
傷口を流水でよく洗ってください	Wash the wound well under running water.
爪で傷口周囲を圧迫し、毒液をしぼり出してください	Use your nails to apply pressure on the stung area and squeeze out the venom.
濡れタオルで傷口を冷やし、安静にしてください	Cool the wound with a wet towel and rest.

▶ヘビに咬まれたら

毒蛇に咬まれると、咬まれた部分が腫れ、強く痛みますよ	When bitten by a venomous snake, the bitten area will swell and be very painful.
傷病者を落ち着かせ、安静にさせてください	Calm down the wounded and put them at rest.
咬まれた部位を心臓より高くしないように	Avoid elevating bitten areas above the heart.
あなたを咬んだ蛇は毒蛇なので、すぐに病院に行って血清を打ってもらう必要があります	The snake that bit you is venomous, so we should take you to a hospital to get the antivenom as soon as possible.

Chapter 6

防災意識を高める

火災予防

▶ 防災施設などの確認をさせる

ご自宅に消火器はありますか？	Do you have a fire extinguisher at home?
消火器の使用期限が切れていないか、確認してください	Please make sure your fire extinguisher hasn't expired.
火災報知機は、ちゃんと作動しますか？	Is your smoke detector working properly?
火災報知機やスプリンクラーは、作動するか定期的に点検してください	Periodically check your smoke detectors and fire sprinklers to make sure they're functioning properly.

▶ 火災予防運動

町内会の夜警に、あなたも参加しませんか？	Could we sign you up to be on the night watch in this neighborhood?
「火の用心！」は、「火元に気をつけましょう」という意味です	"Hi No Yojin!" means "Take precautions against fires."
マッチ1本、火事の元	Just one match can start a fire.
3月1日から7日は春の火災予防運動週間です	March 1 to March 7 is Fire Preparedness Week.
防火管理講習に参加してください	You have to take part in the Fire Marshalling course.
	☑ 会社の指示などで。

今日は空気が乾燥しているので、火事が発生しやすくなっていますよ	The air is very dry today, so there is a greater possibility of fires breaking out.
まだ火が消えていませんよ。ちゃんと消してください	This fire's still burning, so please finish putting it out.
寝たばこは危険です	Smoking in bed is dangerous.
夜、暖房をつけたまま寝ないよう気をつけましょう	Please do not leave your space heaters on at night while you sleep.
キャンドルやお香に火をつけたまま部屋を離れるのは危険ですよ	Stepping out of a room with candles or incense lit is very dangerous.
ガスコンロの火を使っているときはその場を離れないでください	Do not step away from a lit gas stove.
コンセントの接続部にほこりが溜まると、そこから出火する場合があるんですよ	If there's too much dust on the outlets, sparks can form.
子どもに火遊びをさせないように。花火には必ず大人が付き添いましょう	Do not allow your children to play with fire. When using fireworks, make sure there's an adult present.
近所で連続放火事件が発生しています。燃えやすいものを放置しないでください	There have been repeated reports of arson incidents in this neighborhood. Do not leave flammables unattended.

防災意識を高める

台風対策

▶台風の情報を伝える

今週末、大型台風が関東地方を直撃します	A huge typhoon will hit the Kanto Region this weekend.
今夜9時ごろに、最も雨や風が強くなるそうですよ	We'll see the most rain and wind around 9:00 tonight.
この辺りの最大瞬間風速は50m/sを超えるでしょう	The maximum wind speed in this area will surpass 50 meters per second.
今回の台風は速度が遅いので、相当量の雨が降るでしょうね	This typhoon is moving slowly, so there may be large amounts of rain.

▶アドバイスする

ラジオやテレビの台風情報をチェックしましょう	Listen to information about the typhoon on the radio or TV.
暴風が吹いているので、外出は控えたほうがいいですよ	Violent winds are blowing. You shouldn't go outside.
傘がさせないくらいの風なので、気をつけてください	It'll be difficult to use an umbrella in this wind, so be careful.
風で飛ばされる可能性があるので、ベランダの植木鉢は屋内へ移動させたほうがいいですよ	If you have any potted plants on your balcony, bring them in because they can be blown off by these winds.

水難事故や水害の予防

水難事故や水害の予防

ここは遊泳禁止です	Swimming is prohibited here.
この海岸の中央付近は、大変危険な「離岸流」が発生します	Near the middle of this beach, there is a very dangerous rip current. ☑ 離岸流は、海岸の波打ち際から沖合に向かってできる幅10mほどの強い引き潮です。
海や川で釣りをする場合、念のためにライフベストを着用すべきです	If you're going to go fishing in the ocean or in rivers, you should wear a life vest just in case.
この川は浅そうですが、実は岸から50センチほどのところで、急に深くなります	This river looks shallow, but actually, the bottom gets much deeper 50 centimeters from the riverbank.

水害への日常対策

排水溝の掃除をしておきましょう	Let's clean out the drain ditch.
雨どいを点検し、必要なら補修しておきましょう	Be sure to inspect your rain gutters and repair them if needed.
その川は過去に氾濫したことがあるので、豪雨の際には避難することも考えてください	That river has overflowed in the past, so consider evacuating in the event of heavy rains.
冠水している道路を歩いて避難する場合は、長靴よりも、スニーカーのほうがいいそうですよ	If you have to evacuate using roads that are submerged in water, it's better to wear sneakers than rain boots. ☑ 長靴は水が入ってしまうと動けなくなるため、脱げないようにひもで固定できるスニーカーのほうがよいとされています。

防災意識を高める

防犯

▶ 空き巣対策

外出時は施錠してください	Please lock the door when you go out.
砂利を敷くと音が出るので、住居侵入予防に効果がありますよ	Laying gravel is an effective way to prevent home invasions since it makes noise when stepped on.
人感センサー付き照明器具を設置していますか？	Do you have any lights equipped with motion-sensors installed?
防犯サムターンのドア錠に取り替えたほうがいいですよ	You should change your door locks to anti-thumb-turn locks. ☑「サムターン回し」を防止します。

▶ スリ・ひったくり対策

カバンは斜めがけすると、ひったくられにくいですよ	Wearing your bag across your chest makes it harder to be taken away.
自転車のかごには、ひったくり防止カバーを取り付けましょう	Put a cover over your bicycle's basket to prevent theft.
歩きながらスマホを使ったり、イヤホンで音楽を聴いていたりすると狙われやすいですよ	You're more likely to be attacked on the street if you're using your smartphone or listening to music with earphones while walking.
カバンの口が開いていますよ。混み合った電車内では	Your bag is open. You should be careful in crowded trains.

車上荒らし対策

車の中に貴重品は置かないでください	Don't keep valuables in your car.
何も入ってなくてもカバンを車内に置きっぱなしにしないように	You shouldn't leave your bag in your car, even if there's nothing in it.
車には、なんらかの防犯装置をつけましょう	Install some sort of security device on your car.
人通りのない薄暗い路上に駐車するのは危険ですよ	It's dangerous to park in dark areas where there aren't any people around.

子どもの安全・防犯

万一のために、お子さんには防犯ブザーを持たせるといいですよ	It's a good idea to give your children a personal alarm just in case.
近所の方と仲良くなっておくと、いざというときに子供を守ってもらえるかもしれません	If you become friends with your neighbors, they may help protect your children someday.
知らない人に名前を呼ばれて話しかけられても、決してついていかないように言い聞かせておきましょう	Tell your children that, even if someone calls them by their name and tries to talk to them, they should never follow strangers.
留守番する際は、知らない人が訪ねてきても、ドアを開けないように言い聞かせておきましょう	Tell your children not to open the door for strangers when they're home alone.

地震に対する備え（友人や知人との会話）

▶防災グッズ

非常用持ち出し袋を準備しておくといいですよ	You should prepare a survival kit in case of emergencies.
懐中電灯や携帯ラジオの用意も忘れずに	Don't forget to have a flashlight and portable radio ready.
ソーラー充電器を持っておくといいかもしれません	It might be a good idea to have a solar-powered battery charger.
非常食や非常水の賞味期限を定期的にチェックしましょう	Check the expiration dates on emergency food and beverages periodically.
建物から避難する時は、この防災頭巾を頭にかぶるんですよ	You have to put this fireproof hood over your head when you evacuate a building.

▶避難経路

非常階段は、廊下の突き当たりです	The emergency stairs are at the end of the hallway.
エレベーターは止まる可能性があるので、階段を使ってください	The elevators may be stopped, so use the stairs.
この緑の標識は「非常口」を表しています	This green sign indicates an emergency exit.
火災発生時には、ベランダの避難はしごを使ってください	If a fire starts, use the escape ladder out on the balcony.

揺れを感じたら、机の下に潜るように	If it starts shaking, get under a desk.
揺れがおさまったら、最寄の安全な出口を探そう	Once the shaking stops, try to find the nearest safe exit.
それほど大きな揺れでない場合は、まず火の始末をすることが重要です	If it's not shaking too hard, the first and most important thing to do is to put out the fire.
倒れそうなものを押さえる前に、自分の身を守ることが大切ですよ	Protect yourself before trying to keep things from falling over.
暗闇では、割れた窓ガラスでケガをしないように気をつけましょう	Be careful not to hurt yourself on broken glass from the windows when moving in the dark.

ケガの防止

頭にものが落ちてきそうなところに寝ないように	Try not to sleep under places where things may fall on your head.
食器棚の中身が飛び出してくることもあるので、注意しましょう	Things may shoot out the kitchen cabinets, so please be careful.
子ども部屋には背の低い家具だけを置くといいですよ	You should only put low furniture in children's rooms.
屋根瓦が落ちてくる可能性があるので、あわてて戸外に飛び出さないように	Roof tiles may fall down, so don't run out carelessly from your house.

防災意識を高める

高層階での地震は、揺れ始めは遅く、その後激しくなります	On upper floors, earthquakes start slowly, then shake violently.
この住宅は旧耐震基準で建てられているので、耐震診断をしてもらったほうがいいかもしれませんよ	This house was constructed before the antiseismic standards were raised, so you'd better have it tested for seismic resistance.
このマンションは、免震構造になっています	This apartment building is a quake-absorbing structure.
火災が起きた場合、この建物はあっと言う間に燃え尽きますよ	If there's ever a fire, this building would burn down very quickly.
このアパートは耐火性に優れた木材を使っています	This apartment is made from highly fire-resistant timber.

▶家屋への影響

耐震基準を満たしているとは言っても、壁にヒビが入ったりすることはあるでしょう	Even if the construction meets antiseismic standards, the walls may still crack.
配管が壊れることも考えられます	It's also very possible that pipes may burst.
近隣で火災が起った場合、ここにも簡単に燃え移るでしょう	If a fire breaks out next door, it can easily spread to here.

揺れを感じると自動的にガスが停止するようになっています	The gas is set to automatically stop as soon as it detects seismic activity.
家具は固定しておいたほうがいいですよ	It's a good idea to affix furniture so that it won't move.
耐震補強はしていますか？ 自治体から補助金が出ますよ	Have you already done some antiseismic reinforcement? The local government provides monetary assistance for that.
消火器には有効期限があるんですよ	Fire extinguishers have expiration dates.
家電製品のそばに花瓶や水槽を置かないようにしましょう	Try not to put any flower vases or fish tanks near electrical devices.
コンセント部分に水がかかると発火する恐れがあります	If water falls on the outlet, it could ignite.
観音開きの扉にはストッパーを取り付け、中身が飛び出さないようにしておきましょう	For all double-doored cabinets, be sure to place a stopper on the hinge so that things don't shoot out.
石油ストーブのそばには洗濯物やカーテンなど燃えやすいものを置かないように	Make sure that laundry, curtains and other flammable items are away from oil heaters.
ガラス扉にはガラス飛散防止フィルムを貼っておきましょう	You can line glass windows with shatterproof film.

防災意識を高める

停電に備えて、懐中電灯と電池を用意しておきましょう	Keep a flashlight and batteries handy in case of a blackout.
乾電池式の懐中電灯は、点灯するかどうか定期的にチェックしたほうがいいですよ	Periodically check your battery-powered flashlights to make sure they're working.
手回しハンドル充電式の懐中電灯も売っていますよ	They also sell emergency crank flashlights.
懐中電灯と携帯ラジオが一体になったタイプもあります	There are also flashlight radios.
カセット式のガスコンロもあると便利ですよ	Portable gas stoves also come in handy.
飲料水は1人1日2リットルとし、3日分を保管しておきましょう	Try to keep three days worth of drinking water stored away. You should have two liters per day, per person.
水が不要なトイレグッズを常備しておくと、いざというときに役に立つでしょう	Toiletries that don't require water are good to have ready just in case.
水さえあれば保存食を温められるグッズがあります	You can heat up preservable foods with some items that only require water.
LPガスは個別に設置されているため、前回の大震災のときも比較的早く復旧したんです	LP gas units have been individually installed, so even during the last earthquake disaster, we were able to make a relatively quick recovery.

この建物は地震保険に入っていますか？	Does this building have earthquake insurance?
家財も補償の対象となりますよ	You will be reimbursed for your lost household belongings.
火災保険と地震保険はセットで加入するのが一般的です	It's normal to get both fire and earthquake insurance together in a package deal.
地震によって起こった火災については、火災保険は補償しないそうです　☑「地震保険」から支払われます。	It seems that fire insurance does not cover any fires that are started due to earthquakes.
地震保険の内容は、どの保険会社のものでも変わりないそうです	It seems that the details of earthquake insurance are the same at every insurance company.

家族との連絡

非常時の家族の集合場所を決めておくといいですよ	You should prepare a meeting place for your family in case you get separated during an emergency.
家族が離ればなれで被災した場合、自分の身の安全をまず確保してから、家族の安否を確認しましょう	If you and your family get separated during a disaster, first ensure your own safety, then make sure your family is safe.
災害用伝言板サービスの活用方法を確認しておきましょう	Be sure to familiarize yourself with how to use emergency message board services.
家のどこが一番安全かを話し合っておくといいですよ	You should talk about where the safest areas in your house are.

防災意識を高める

地震に対する備え（学校）

▶ 防災グッズと AED

椅子にかけている防災頭巾は、地震などで避難する時にかぶって、頭を保護するためのものです	The disaster hood hanging from that chair is meant to protect your head when evacuating during disasters, such as earthquakes.
この学校には生徒全員が1週間過ごせる量の非常食が備蓄されています	At this school, we have enough emergency food supplies in storage to sustain each student for a week.
このひもを引っ張ると大きな音がでます	If you pull this cord, it emits a loud siren. ☑ 防犯ブザーの説明です。
電気ショックを与えることによって、心臓を正常なリズムに戻します	By giving electrical shocks, the heart reestablishes an effective rhythm.

▶ 避難経路

校庭に逃げるときは、この狭い階段ではなく、中央階段を使いましょう	When escaping out to the schoolyard, avoid these narrow stairways and use the main stairs.
廊下の突き当たりにある非常階段は、普段は使用してはいけませんよ	The emergency stairs located at the end of hallways are not for regular use.
校舎の2階の非常ドアを開けると、高台へ続く通路があります	If you use the emergency exit doors on the second floor, you can find a passageway that leads to higher ground. ☑「津波」を想定した避難経路
この地図の線は、避難経路を示しています	The lines on this map indicate the evacuation route.

地震が発生したら、勝手な行動はせずに、先生の指示に従ってください	In the event of an earthquake, avoid going off on your own and follow your teacher's instructions.
「押さない」「駆けない」「しゃべらない」「戻らない」という約束を守ってください	Honor the following code: No pushing, no rushing, no talking and no going back.
地震が発生したら、机の下にもぐり、机の脚につかまってください	If there's an earthquake, get under your desks and hold on to the desk legs.
まず頭部を保護してください	Protect your head before anything else.

▶登下校中の危険性

ブロック塀、看板、自動販売機から離れるように	Distance yourself from concrete-block walls, large signs and vending machines as much as possible.
学校まで距離があるなら、近くの空き地や公園に避難してください	If the school is too far, please evacuate to the nearest park or open area.
揺れがおさまったら、学校か自宅、近いほうへ移動してください	Once the earthquake stops, go home or to school; whichever closer.
電車やバスでは、柱やつり革にしっかりつかまり、急停車のショックから身を守りましょう	On a bus or train, protect yourself from sudden stops by holding on tightly to the safety handles.

防災意識を高める

▶教室別の危険性

図書室では、本棚のそばから離れてください	In the library, keep away from the bookshelves.
音楽室では、ピアノのそばから離れてください	In the music room, keep away from the piano.
廊下の窓ガラスが割れたり、下駄箱やロッカーが倒れてくることがあります	The hallway windows could break, and shoe racks and lockers could fall over.
揺れを感じたら、ちゅうちょせずにドアは少し開けておきましょう	If you feel shaking, do not hesitate to open the door slightly.
体育館にいたら、真ん中に腰を下ろして頭を守りましょう	In the gym, remain seated in the center and cover your head.
技術室では、電動のこぎりなどの動力機器からすぐに離れましょう	In the art room, get away from electric saws and other machinery immediately.
給食の配膳中に地震が発生した場合は、やけどに注意し、身を守りましょう	If an earthquake happens during lunch time preparation, avoid burn injuries and take cover.
サッカーゴールが倒れてくることも考えられます	The soccer goal could fall over.

津波は地震から数分遅れてやってくることを覚えておいてください	Please remember that a tsunami arrives a few minutes after an earthquake.
大きな地震の場合、ものは落ちるだけでなく、あなためがけて飛んでくることがあります	In a large earthquake, objects will not only fall but may fly at you.
大きな地震の後には余震が発生するので、注意が必要です	Aftershocks will take place after large earthquakes, so be careful.
過去の震災では、地震による火事もまた多くの命を奪いました	In past disasters, fires caused by earthquakes also claimed many lives.
１メートルの津波でも軽視してはいけません。巻き込まれれば死ぬ可能性は十分にあります	Do not underestimate a one meter high tsunami. Getting caught in a tsunami wave is life-threatening.
地震は突然やってきます。地震はそう簡単に予知できません	Earthquakes happen unexpectedly. They aren't easily predictable.
津波にのまれると方向感覚が失われ、簡単に浮かび上がることはできなくなります	Once swallowed up by a tsunami, your sense of direction is lost, making it difficult to rise to the surface.
津波は川を遡上することがあります	A tsunami wave could reverse water flow and move upriver.

防災意識を高める

地震に対する備え（オフィス）

▶ 備えと避難経路

消火器の場所を確認しておきましょう	Confirm the location of fire extinguishers.
非常用物品は、各自のロッカー内に保管してください ☑ 取り出しやすく、被害を受けにくい場所を選ぶのが原則	Keep emergency use items in your locker.
保管できない物品の調達先企業一覧表は、ここに掲示しておきます	For items that cannot be stored, there is a list of procurement companies on the bulletin board.
冬には、タオルや携帯カイロをロッカーに入れておくと役立ちます	Keeping a small towel or heating pad in your locker is very convenient in the winter.
従業員全員分の非常用寝具は用意されておりません	We don't have enough emergency sleeping supplies for everyone on staff.
仕事場から一時避難場所までの経路は、各自この地図で確認しておいてください	Everyone, please be sure to look at this map and check the route to the temporary evacuation area near the office.
非常口のそばにものを置かないでください	Do not put anything in the way of the emergency exits.
避難経路や非常階段に障害物がないかどうか定期的に点検しましょう	Conduct periodic checks of the evacuation route and emergency stairs to make sure there aren't any obstructions.

常日頃から整理整頓をしておきましょう	Let's make it a habit to be neat and tidy at all times.
コンロの自動消火装置が正しく機能するか確認しておきましょう	Always check to see if the auto-shutoff function is working on your gas stove.
移動、転倒、落下の危険があるオフィス家具に気がついたら、私に報告してください	If you notice any office furniture in positions prone to falling, slipping or coming off, please let me know.
「情報連絡担当」や「避難誘導担当」などの任務分担を決めます	We'll be assigning one person to be an "Information Officer" and another to be an "Evacuation Leader."

地震発生直後の行動

動きやすくて丈夫なスニーカーに履き替えましょう	Change into comfortable and durable sneakers.
窓ガラスが割れることがあるので、窓際から離れましょう	Keep away from the windows because the glass could break.
OA機器の落下に気をつけましょう	Be careful of falling office appliances.
手すりがある場合には、それにつかまり姿勢を低くしてください	If there is a handle, hold it firmly and crouch down.

この建物の耐震性は問題ありません	The seismic resistance of this building should not be a problem.
この建物は、震度6で倒壊する恐れがあります	A level 6 earthquake could destroy this building.
来月から耐震補強工事を行います	From next month, seismic strengthening construction will take place.
耐震診断の手配をお願いします	Please arrange for this building to get evaluated for earthquake resistance.
現在、耐震補強工事の見積もりを依頼しています	We are now requesting an estimate for the seismic strengthening construction.

▶ライフライン断絶への備え

停電になると、非常灯が自動的に点灯します	In a power outage, emergency lights will switch on automatically.
6年保存可能な水を保管しています	We keep water with a storage life of six years.
他の情報伝達手段よりも、インターネットは災害に強いと言われています	Compared to other means of communication, it is said that the Internet is more resilient to big disasters.
ライフラインの復旧には時間がかかります	The restoration of all utilities will take time.

ことえバスやタクシーに乗れたとしても、道は大渋滞になることが予想されます	Even if buses and taxis are available, heavy road congestion is predicted.
建物が倒れて道を塞いでしまう可能性もあります	There is a possibility that buildings will fall and block the roads.
むやみに移動する必要はありません。ここで一夜を過ごす準備をしましょう	There is no need to wander around. Let's make preparations to stay the night here.
「災害時帰宅支援ステーション」のステッカーが貼ってある店舗は、水道水、トイレ、情報、休憩の場を提供します	Shops with a "Support Spot For Disaster Victims Unable To Go Home" sticker offer tap water, toilets, information and places to rest.
ときどき休憩をとり、体力を温存することも必要です	It is important to take periodic breaks and save your strength.
トイレは混雑して使えなくなるかもしれません	Bathrooms could become overcrowded and unavailable.
自分用の帰宅地図を作っておきましょう	Make your own map to use when going home.

防災意識を高める

地震に対する備え（公共）

▶ 歩道

地震中は、ガラス張りの建物から離れたほうがいいですよ	During an earthquake, it's best to distance yourself from glass-sided buildings.
電柱や自動販売機が倒れてくることがあります	Telephone poles and vending machines could fall over.
オフィスビルの割れた窓ガラスは時速40〜60キロで落下します	Fallen glass from office building windows can fall at a speed of 40 to 60 kilometers.
エアコンの室外機、花のプランターが落下してくることがあります	Outdoor air conditioning units and flower pots could fall.

▶ 交通機関

停車後は、乗務員の指示に従いましょう	Obey the crew's instructions after coming to a complete stop.
地震の際の線路への転落を防ぐため、ホームでは黄色い線の内側を歩くように	In order to avoid falling onto the train tracks during an earthquake, be sure to walk on the inside of the yellow lines on the platform.
急停車する可能性があるので、高速バスの車内ではシートベルトをしましょう	The high-way bus may have to make sudden stops, so wear your seat belts.

バッグや買い物か
ごで頭を保護し、
ショーケースなど倒
れやすいものから離
れましょう

Protect your head with a bag or shopping basket and move away from display cases or other things that could fall over.

小さい子供を連れて
いる場合には、子
供をしっかりと抱
き寄せて、ジャ
ケットなどで頭を
保護してあげま
しょう

If accompanying a small child, hold them tightly and protect their head with a jacket or other object.

もしはぐれたら、
外の駐車場で落ち
合おう

If we get separated, meet in the outdoor parking lot.

地下街

火災が発生しなけ
れば比較的安全で
す

It's relatively safe as long as a fire doesn't start.

停電になっても、
非常照明がつくま
でむやみに動かな
いようにしましょ
う

In a power outage, stay where you are until the emergency lights come on.

地下街では60メー
トルごとに非常口
が設置されてます

In underground shopping centers, emergency exits are located every 60 meters.

壁づたいに歩いて
避難してください

Please evacuate by walking along the wall.

防災意識を高める

▶映画館・劇場など

座席の間に身を隠して、揺れが収まるのを待ちましょう	Please get under your seats and wait until the shaking stops.
停電しても誘導灯や非常灯がつきますので、慌てずに係員の指示に従いましょう	Even during a blackout, the emergency and guide lights will come on, so keep calm and follow the instructions of the staff.
慌てて出口や階段に殺到しないようにしましょう	Don't panic and try not to rush out the exits or stairs.
天井からの落下物に注意しましょう	Be careful of items falling from the ceiling.

▶エレベーター・エスカレーター

エレベーターに閉じこめられても、落ち着いて「非常用呼び出しボタン」を押して助けを呼びましょう	If you get trapped in an elevator, don't panic and try calling for help by pushing the "Emergency Call Button."
救助にすぐに駆けつけてくれるとは限りません	Help may not come right away.
エスカレーターに乗るときは普段から手すりに手を掛けて乗るようにしてください ☑ 急停止したときの「将棋倒し事故」を防ぐためです。	Please make a habit of holding on to the handrail when using escalators.

災害の危険性を地域別に説明する

海沿いの地域

大地震の後には、津波がやってくる可能性があります	After a large earthquake, there is a possibility of a tsunami hitting.
津波は繰り返し襲って来て、第一波の後にさらに高い波が来ることもあります	Tsunamis come in waves, after the first wave, the following waves may be larger.
いったん波が引いても絶対に戻ってはいけません	Even if the tide recedes, do not go back.
地震発生直後に津波の第一波が到達することもあります	There are also times when the first wave of a tsunami hits right after an earthquake hits.

川岸

津波は川をさかのぼってくるので、川沿いの地域も津波に注意する必要があります	The tsunami can spill over to the rivers, so people in riverfront areas also need to be alert to tsunamis.
流れに沿って上流に避難しても、津波が遡上してくる可能性があります	If you try to seek shelter upstream in the direction of the current, there's a possibility of the tsunami coming your way.
流れに対して直角方向にすばやく逃げましょう	Try to stay perpendicular to the current and escape quickly.

防災意識を高める

地震によって、地盤のゆるい土地では液状化現象が起こることがあります	Some earthquakes can cause soil liquefaction in softer areas of land.
液状化により、建物が沈下したり傾いたりすることがあります	Liquefaction can cause buildings to sink or tilt sideways.
あなたが住んでいる土地が埋立地なら、液状化のリスクが高いということになります	If your residence was built on a landfill, the risk of liquefaction is very high.
「液状化マップ」とは、液状化のしやすさ・しにくさを地図上に色分けして示したものです	A liquefaction map color codes areas that have high and low liquefaction risks.

▶住宅密集地帯

木造住宅が密集している地域では、火が燃え広がりやすくなります	Fires spread quickly in areas where wooden houses are close together.
幅が狭く、曲がりくねった道では、消火や救助活動が困難になります	Fire fighting and other relief efforts become difficult on narrow and winding roads.
特に東京の下町は倒壊しやすい木造住宅が密集しています	The old residential area of Tokyo in particular is full of easily destroyable wooden buildings.

ここは海抜が低いので、洪水危険地域です	This is a flood danger area due to its low elevation level.
超高層ビルの多くは大きく揺れることによって地震の衝撃を吸収します	Many high-rise buildings sway a lot to absorb the shock of earthquakes.
立っていられないほど大きく揺れることがあります	Sometimes it shakes so forcefully that you can't even stand.

山・土砂災害危険個所

落石から身を守りましょう	Watch out for falling rocks.
崖や急傾斜地には近づかないようにしましょう	Keep away from cliffs and steep slopes.
住んでいる場所が「土砂災害危険箇所」かどうか確認しましょう	Check if your residential area is a landslide risk area.
雨が降り出したら土砂災害警戒情報に注意しましょう	If it starts to rain, be alert for landslide warning notices.
各都道府県が「土砂災害危険箇所」と「土砂災害危険区域」を公開しています。ウェブで検索してみてください	All municipalities have released maps for "landslide-prone spots" and "landslide-prone areas." Look them up online.

▶ 寒冷地・豪雪地帯

この地域は、冬にはかなりの積雪量があるので、冬用タイヤの準備をしておく必要がありますよ	This area gets a lot of snow, so you have to be ready to switch to snow tires in the winter.
冬が来る前に、除雪用の道具をそろえておいたほうがいいですよ	Be sure to stock up on snow shoveling gear before winter comes.
麓は暖かくても、山の上の方はまだ雪が残っているので、タイヤチェーンを持っていくといいですよ	Even if it's warm down on the foothills, up in the mountains, there may still be a lot of snow, so keep some snow chains handy.

▶ 原発周辺

ラジオやテレビ、インターネットで常に、事故についての情報を集めてください	Always stay informed about incidents by using a radio, TV or the Internet.
ここは原発の20キロ圏内なので、いつでも避難できる準備をしておく必要があります	This location is within 20 kilometers of a nuclear power plant, so it's important to be ready to evacuate at any time.
原発の30キロ圏内にお住まいなら、避難指示の前に自主避難することも考えておきましょう	If you live within 30 kilometers of a nuclear power plant, get ready to evacuate on your own before receiving evacuation instructions.

避難訓練

これらが防災センターです	These are disaster prevention centers.
ただ今、1階にて火災訓練が行われています	A fire drill is taking place on the first floor.
お客様は、係員の指示に従い避難してください	Customers, please follow evacuation instructions from staff.
近いうちに抜き打ちで避難訓練を行います	We will be holding a surprise emergency drill in the coming days.
地下3階から2階、および25階から32階の避難訓練参加者は避難を開始してください	Emergency drill participants on floors B3 and B2 and floors 25 to 32 please begin evacuation.
避難指示がない階の訓練参加者は、該当する階の指示があるまでお待ちください	Participants on floors without evacuation instructions, please wait on a corresponding floor with instructions.
初期消火班は直ちに消火作業を開始。避難誘導班は誘導配置につけ	Initial fire extinguishing squad, please begin operations. Evacuation guidance squad, begin making arrangements.
ただ今、マイクのテスト中。これから避難訓練を行います	This is a mic test. We will now hold an emergency drill.

防災意識を高める

東日本大震災を思い出してください。訓練ではなく本番だと思って、取り組んでください	Don't forget the great disaster in Tohoku. Think of this as the real thing, not as a drill.
ヘルメットをかぶってください。全員かぶりましたか？	You have to wear a hard hat. Does everyone have one on?
1人ずつ脱出用シュートに入ってください	Only one person can go down the emergency evacuation chute at a time.
キムさん、この避難はしごを降ろしてくれますか	Kim, can you release the fire escape ladder?

▶学校

揺れがおさまったら、落ち着いて校庭に避難してください	Once the shaking has stopped, proceed to the schoolyard in an orderly fashion.
これは訓練です。訓練です。地震が発生しました。生徒は教職員の誘導に従いグラウンドに避難してください	This is a drill. This is a drill. There has been an earthquake. We ask all students to please follow behind your teachers and evacuate to the playground.
教職員は、生徒を避難場所へ誘導し、点呼を行ってください	We ask that the faculty lead the students to the evacuation site and take a head count.
クラスごとに1列に並んでください	Please line up by homeroom.

他のテナント企業と合同で避難訓練を行います	We will conduct evacuation drills together with other businesses that share our building.
各部の代表者は人員点呼を行い、避難状況を本部へ報告してください	A representative from each department will take roll of their personnel and report their situation to headquarters.
事前に連絡した通り、ジョーンズさんには誘導係になっていただきます	As previously stated, Jones will be in charge of leading everyone.
どうしても外せない仕事があるため、山本さんは不参加です	Mr. Yamamoto will be unable to join us due to work-related issues that require his attention.

消火訓練

消防署の方が消火訓練に協力してくださります	Some people from the fire department will be assisting in the fire extinguishing training.
誰か消火訓練をやってみませんか？	Would anyone like to try fire extinguishing training?
火元に消火器を向けましょう	Try to aim the fire extinguisher at the base of the fire.
消火器は炎から3〜6メートル離れたところから使用してください	Stand three to six meters away from the fire when using the fire extinguisher.
安全ピンを抜いてください	Remove the pin.

ホースを火元に向けてください	Aim the hose at the base of the fire.
レバーを強く握ってください	Squeeze the lever.
火が完全に消えたかどうか、確認してください	Make sure that the fire has been completely extinguished.
ホースの片づけを手伝ってください	Please help with putting away the fire hoses.

▶反省会

エレベーターを利用しましたね。たとえエレベーターが動いていたとしても、絶対に乗ってはいけません	You used the elevator. Even if the elevators are running, don't get on them.
避難が遅い部署がありました。アナウンスがあったらすぐに行動しましょう	Some departments were late to the drill. Start moving as soon as you hear the announcements.
訓練中、私語が目立ちました。次回は、もっとまじめに取り組んでください	We noticed that many people were chatting during the drill. You must take the drill seriously next time.
10分以内に全員避難しないといけないのですが、今回は15分もかかってしまいました	We're supposed to be able to fully evacuate within 10 minutes, but this time, it took at least 15.

Appendix

災害時に役立つ資料集

緊急時のとっさのひと言フレーズ

▶助けを求める
- -

Help!	助けて
Somebody help me, please!	誰か助けて
I need help.	助けてください
Come quick!	早く来て
Somebody call the police!	誰か警察を呼んで
Somebody call a doctor!	誰かお医者さんを呼んで
I've been shot!	(銃で) 撃たれた！
I just got hit by a car!	車にはねられました

▶緊急事態を告げる
- -

Emergency!	緊急事態です！
Earthquake!	地震だ！
Fire!	火事だ！
Firestorm!	火災旋風だ！
Landslide!	地滑りだ！
*Avalanche!	雪崩だ！ (* 発音はアヴァランチ)
Tsunami!	津波だ！
The building is on fire!	ビルが火事だ！
The water is rising!	水位が上がっているぞ！
There's smoke everywhere!	そこらじゅう、煙だらけだ
The bridge is going to *collapse!	橋が崩れるぞ！ (* 発音はコラップス)

▶避難するよう呼び掛ける
- -

Run!	走れ！
Go!	さあ、早く！
Just run!	とにかく逃げろ！
We've got to get out of here now.	今すぐここを出ない
Head for high ground!	高台へ逃げろ！
Get a move on!	急げ！
Hurry!	急げ！
Run for your lives!	逃げろ！／危ない！
Get into the car!	車の中に入って！
Jump into the water!	水の中に飛び込んで！
We have to jump.	飛び降りよう
It's not safe here.	ここにいたら危険です

Be careful!	気をつけて！
Be on guard!	気をつけて！
Watch out!	気をつけて！　危ない！
Watch your head!	頭上に気をつけて！
Watch your feet!	足元に気をつけて！
Watch your step!	足元に気をつけて！
Behind you!	後ろ！
Do not go outside!	外に出るな！
Don't go in there!	そこに入らないで！
Duck!	ふせろ！
Get down!	ふせろ！
Crawl!	手をついてしゃがんで！
Cover your head!	頭を覆って！

落ち着かせる

Easy!	落ち着いて！
Calm down.	落ち着いて
Don't panic.	動転しないで
Don't worry.	心配しないで
Everything will be fine.	大丈夫だから
Help will be here soon.	すぐ助けが来ますよ
You'll be better soon.	すぐによくなりますよ
We'll be safe here.	ここなら大丈夫です
This should be far enough.	ここまで来ればもう大丈夫ですよ

その他

Need some help?	手伝いましょうか？
Are you okay?	大丈夫ですか？
Are you hurt?	怪我をしていますか？
We'd better stay here.	ここにいたほうがいい
Wait here for help.	ここで救助を待って
Don't move!	じっとしていなさい
Come this way.	こっちに来てください
You're bleeding.	血が出ていますよ
Don't do that!	そんなことしないで！
I'm okay.	私は大丈夫です
Are you lost?	道に迷いましたか？

災害時に役立つ資料集

非常時の英語アナウンス

お店や学校などで、非常時にそのまま活用できる「英語アナウンス」です。なお、冒頭の「呼びかけ」部分は、学校の場合は Attention students and staff, ...「生徒および職員のみなさんに申し上げます」、会社の場合は May I have everyone's attention.「みなさんに申し上げます」、お店の場合は Ladies and gentlemen, your attention please.「お客様にお知らせいたします」などのように変えて用いるといいでしょう。

▶火災報知機のテスト

Ladies and Gentlemen, your attention please. There will now be a test of the building's fire alarm. This is only a test. Please remain where you are. Thank you.

お客様に申し上げます。ただいまより、当ビルの火災報知機のテストを行います。これは単なるテストですので、避難などはなさらないようお願いいたします。

▶火災報知機が作動した場合

The fire alarm has been activated. We are currently investigating the situation, so please remain calm and stand by for further instructions. Thank you.

ただいま、火災報知機が作動いたしました。現在状況の調査を行っておりますので、指示があるまで落ち着いて待機してください。よろしくお願いいたします。

▶火災報知機の誤動作を知らせる

May I have your attention, please? This was a false alarm. I repeat, this was a false alarm. We apologize for the confusion. Thank you.

みなさまにお知らせいたします。ただいまの警報は誤報です。繰り返し申し上げます。誤報です。混乱させてしまい、申し訳ありませんでした。

▶避難の指示

Attention, please. This is an emergency. Please evacuate the building immediately in an orderly fashion using the nearest staircase. Do not use the elevator or escalator. Wait in the designated evacuation zone until given further instructions.

みなさまに申し上げます。緊急事態が発生しました。直ちに、落ち着いて最寄りの階段よりビルの外へ避難してください。エレベータやエスカレーターは使用なさらないでください。指示があるまで、指定された避難エリアにて待機してください。

▶緊急事態が収束したことを知らせる

Ladies and gentlemen, your attention please. The building is now safe for all employees to resume their normal activities. We thank you for your patience.

みなさまに申し上げます。当ビルの緊急事態は収束いたしましたので、全従業員は通常業務を再開してください。ご協力に感謝いたします。

地震が発生した場合

Ladies and gentlemen, your attention please. There has been an earthquake. Please carefully evacuate the building immediately and remain outside until further notice.

みなさまに申し上げます。ただいま地震が発生いたしました。直ちに落ち着いてビルの外へ避難してください。指示があるまで、外にてお待ちください。

津波が発生した場合

Ladies and gentlemen, your attention please. JMA has issued a tsunami warning for the coastal areas between Sendai and Shiogama. Please move to higher ground immediately.

みなさまに申し上げます。気象予報によれば、仙台・塩釜間の沿岸部に津波報が発令しました。直ちに、上の階に移動してください。

ガス漏れ

A gas leak has been detected in the building. Immediately turn off any burners and extinguish open flames, and prepare to evacuate. Please await further instructions.

ビルにおいて、ガス漏れが検知されました。直ちに、ガスコンロや裸火を消火し、避難準備をしてください。さらなる指示があるまで待機していてください。

武装した犯罪者が出現した

Attention students and staff. This is a Code Red lockdown. Please lock all doors and windows and sit quietly. I repeat, this is a Code Red lockdown.

生および職員のみなさんにお知らせします。コード・レッドの避難命令が令されました。ドアや窓をすべて閉め、その場で静かに着席していてください。繰り返します。コード・レッドの避難命令が発令されました。code red「厳戒警報」は、銃撃事件などの重大な事態になったときに発令される、高レベルの警戒警報です。

爆弾が発見された

Attention employees. There has been a bomb threat in the building. Please prepare to evacuate immediately. After evacuation, wait for further instructions from your supervisor.

業員のみなさま、このビルに対して、爆破予告がありました。直ちに避難準備をしてください。避難後は、上司からの指示を待ってください。

災害時に役立つ標識や掲示

▶防災設備などに関する標識や掲示

「非常口」

「非常階段」

「避難経路」

「消火器」

「防火シャッター」

FIRE DOOR KEEP CLOSED DO NOT BLOCK

「防火扉につき解放禁止。前に物を置かないこと」

THIS DOOR IS FOR EMERGENCY USE ONLY

「この扉は非常時以外使用しないでください」

「火事の際はエレベーターではなく階段を使用してください」

被災後に使える標識や掲示

「ガラスの破片に注意」

Sorry... Temporarily Closed

「臨時休業中」

「故障中」

Sorry... Temporarily Out Of Service

「一時的に使用不可」

「おひとり様3個まで」

「この自動扉は故障中です」

We're trying
to save power.
We apologize for
the inconvenience.

「節電中につき、ご不便をおかけいたしております」

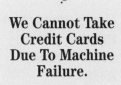

We Cannot Take
Credit Cards
Due To Machine
Failure.

「機械の故障のため、クレジットカードは使えません」

「3年2組集合場所」

「災害対策本部」

「救護室」

「給水所」

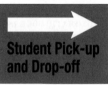

「生徒送迎所」

「危険！ ホットスポットあり」

DO NOT PUSH.
DO NOT RUN.
DO NOT SPEAK.
DO NOT GO BACK.

「押さない、駆けない、喋らない、戻らない」

If you are sick or injured, please see the school nurse.

「体調の悪い人やけがをした人は保健の先生へ申し出てください」

避難所で使える標識や掲示

避難所などで「掲示物」あるいは「サイン」として使える図版を集めてみました。

管理上必要な指示

Keep Out

「立ち入り禁止」

Please Let Us Know When You Go Out

「外出時には声をかけること」

Please Do Not Be Late For Meals

「食事の時間は守りましょう」

All Lights Must Be Turned Off By 10:00PM

「消灯は午後10時です」

Always Be Considerate Of Other Residents

他の居住者の迷惑にならないよう
常にご配慮ください」

Please Do Not Eat Or Drink In This Room

「この部屋での飲食はご遠慮
ください」

Distribution of Donated Clothing Is Scheduled For 2:00 PM

義援品の衣類の配給は午後2時に
行う予定です」

Keep Your Valuables In Your Possession At All Times

「貴重品は常に携行してください」

▶健康や衛生などに関するもの

「禁煙」

「身の回りを清潔に」

「飲用可能」

「この水は飲めません」

「手を洗いましょう」

「使った後はトイレを流しましょう」

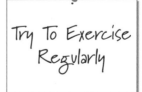

To Prevent
Infectious Diseases,
Please Wear A
Mask

「感染症予防のため、マスクを着用のこと」

Try To Exercise
Regularly

「定期的に運動するように心掛けましょう」

「ここで靴をお脱ぎください」

「この場所では携帯電話の使用はお控えください」

「携帯電話はマナーモードにしてください」

「危険　可燃性につき火気厳禁」

Emergency Assembly Point

「緊急時集合地点」

Information Bulletin Board

「情報掲示板」

Homestay Information

「ホームステイのご案内」

Volunteers Needed

「ボランティア募集中」

「英語通訳サービス利用可」

「無料散髪サービス」

非常用器具の使い方

▶消火器の使い方 How To Use A Fire Extinguisher

1. Carry the extinguisher to the area of fire.
   消火器を火元まで持ち運ぶ

2. Pull out the yellow pin.
   黄色い安全ピンを引き抜く

3. Release the hose from the latch on the body.
   ホースを本体から外す

4. Aim the hose at the base of the fire.
   ホースを火元に向ける

5. Spray the foam by squeezing firmly on the lever.
   レバーを強く握って、消火剤を噴射する

Important points
注意点

・Don't get too close to the flames.
　火元に近づきすぎないようにしましょう。

・Standard powder fire extinguishers spray for about 15 seconds.
　一般的な粉末消火器の場合、噴射時間は15秒程度です。

・If using outdoors, spray with the wind.
　屋外で使用する場合、風上から噴射するようにします。

・"PASS" is an acronym which stands for "Pull, Aim, Squeeze and Sweep." This shows the basic operation of a fire extinguisher: Pull the pin, Aim the nozzle, Squeeze the handle and Sweep the nozzle side to side.

　PASS という略語があり、これは "Pull, Aim, Squeeze and Sweep" を略したものです。「ピンを引き、ノズルを向け、ハンドルを握って、ノズルを横方向に掃くように動かす」という、消火器の基本動作を示したものです。

避難ばしごの使い方 How To Use A Emergency Ladder

1. Open the door to a 90° angle.
   上蓋を 90 度開ける

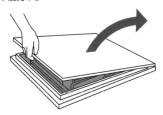

2. After making sure nobody is below you, push down the lever
   with your foot and release the ladder.
   下に人がいないことを確認してから、レバーを足で押し下げ、はしごを
   延ばす

3. After the ladder has completely dropped, carefully climb down
   to safety.
   はしごが下まで伸びきった事を確認してから、落ち着いてはしごを降りて
   避難する

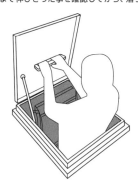

mportant
points
注意点

· If there is a child lock on the door, please disable it.
  蓋に「チャイルドロック」がかかっている場合は、それを解
  除します

· Do not place objects on top of the emergency ladder.
  避難ばしごの上には、荷物などを置かないようにしましょう

▶ 救助袋の使い方 **How To Use An Escape Chute**

1. Detach the top and front panels.
上蓋および前板を取り外す

2. Remove the security belt and drop the sandbag (stone weight) to the ground.
袋を固定しているバンドを外し、砂袋（重し）を地上に投げる

3. Slowly lower the chute to the ground.
袋をゆっくり地上に下ろす

4. Lift up the metal-framed chute entrance to lock it in place and stabilize it.
入口の金具を起こし、固定する

5. Sit with legs inside the chute while holding onto the safety belt.
安全ベルトを持ち、両足をそろえて降下姿勢をとる

6. Drop down the chute with your hands raised and slightly bending your right leg.
降下中は、両手を上げ、右ひざを少し曲げること

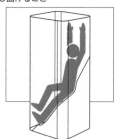

Important points
注意点

· Make sure nobody is below you before throwing the sandbag (stone weight).
砂袋を投下する際には、地上に人がいないか確認しましょ

· When you reach the ground, exit the chute to make way the next person.
次の人のために、地上に着いたら直ちに救助袋から出ましょ

救命胴衣の使い方 How To Use A Life Vest

1. Put your arms through the arm holes and fasten the metal clasp on the front.
救命胴衣に腕を通し、前の金具を止めます

2. Pull the tabs to inflate the vest. If the vest doesn't inflate, blow into the tubes.
ひもを引いて膨らませます。膨らみが足りない場合は、息を吹き込んで調整します

Important points
注意点

The life vest described here is the standard type, but there are other types of inflatable and non-inflatable flotation devices, such as water flotation belts, styrofoam floats, etc., so always remember to check the user's manual.

ここで説明した救命胴衣は標準的なタイプですが、ウエストポーチ型や、発泡スチロールなどで出来た固定式など、様々なタイプがあるので、使用説明書を必ず確認しましょう。

心肺蘇生法 Cardio Pulmonary Resuscitation

1. Check to see if the person is conscious by tapping them on the shoulder and talking to them.
肩を叩きながら声をかけ、意識の有無を確認する

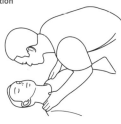

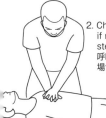

2. Check to see if he or she is breathing, and if not, perform 30 compressions to the sternum.
呼吸があるかどうか確認し、呼吸をしていない場合は、胸骨圧迫を 30 回行う

胸骨圧迫は胸の真ん中

3. After applying pressure to the sternum, give rescue breathing. Give two breaths for one second each, and breathe with enough air to raise their chest.
胸骨圧迫後、人工呼吸を行う。胸が上がる程度の息を、約1秒かけて、2回吹き込む

Important points
注意点

· If rescue breathing cannot be performed, continue applyin compressions to the sternum instead.
人工呼吸の実施がためらわれる場合、人工呼吸を行わず、骨圧迫を続けます

· As a first step, ask someone nearby to call an ambulance o find an AED.
まずは、周囲の人に声をかけ、救急車を呼んでもらったら AEDを探してきてもらいましょう

▶ AED（自動体外式除細動器）の使い方
How To Use An AED (Automated External Defibrillator)

1. Turn the AED on.
AEDの電源を入れる

2. Remove the person's clothing and, following the audio instructions from the AED, apply the pads.
相手の衣服を脱がせ、音声の指示に従ってパッドを装着する

3. Connect the pads to the AED. The AED will start to automatically analyze the person's heart rhythm. To ensure that the AED operates properly, make sure no one is touching the person.
パッドと AED を接続する。自動的に心電図の読み取りが始まるので、誤作動防止のため、患者から手を離すこと

4. If the AED advised that defibrillation is needed, press the blinking button to engage defibrillation. To avoid shock, make sure that no one is touching the person.
「ショックが必要です」とのメッセージがあった場合、点滅しているボタンを押すと、除細動が行われる。感電防止のため、必ず患者から手を離すこと

5. After the defibrillations have stopped, begin cardiac massage if the AED instructs that it is needed.
除細動完了後、機械から指示があれば、心臓マッサージを開始する

Important points
注意点

· Methods of operation may differ from one AED to another.
機械によって使用方法が若干異なる場合があります

· When applying pads, be sure to wipe away any sweat or moisture with a towel or cloth.
パッドを貼る際、汗などで肌が濡れている場合は、タオルなどで拭き取ります

· If the first defibrillation does not resuscitate the person, further shock may be needed.
1回目の除細動で蘇生しなかった場合、再度ショックを加えることもあります

▶ 屋内消火栓（2号消火栓）の使い方　How To Use A Fire Hose (Type II)

1. Open the valve and the pump will activate automatically.
   バルブを解放すると、ポンプが自動的に起動する

2. Holding the nozzle, pull out the hose and move to the flames.
   ノズルを持って、ホースを伸ばしながら、火元に向かいます

3. Turn the nozzle valve to release the water.
   ノズルについているコックを開き、放水します

Important points
注意点

・Type-I Fire Hoses require two people to operate; Type-II Fire Hoses can be operated by one person.
1号消火栓は2人で操作する必要がありますが、2号消火栓は1人で使用することができます。

・Methods of operation may differ from one fire hose to another.
使用方法は消火栓によって異なる場合があります。

外国人に教えたい！緊急時に頼れる情報サービス

テレビ・ラジオの外国語放送

テレビ

NHK の総合テレビでは、下記の時間、英語の副音声でニュースを視聴できます。

午前7時～午前8時
正午～午後1時
午後7時～午後8時
午後9時～午後10時

上記以外の時間帯では、「NHK ワールド TV」（ケーブルテレビのチャンネル）で英語放送を視聴できます。

ラジオ

□ NHK ラジオ第2放送
地震などの災害発生を知らせる緊急警報放送や津波注意報・津波警報・大津波警報を英語・韓国語・中国語・ポルトガル語の4言語で放送しています。
＊各地の周波数は、NHK のホームページでご確認ください。

□ AFN（American Forces Network）
東京 810kHz

□ InterFM
東京 76.1MHz

Disaster Emergency Message Dial（災害用伝言ダイヤル）

This phone number is for a service that people can use to find out if their family members or friends are safe by leaving a voice recorded message or checking messages left for them.（これは録音メッセージを残したり、聞くことによって、家族や友人がお互いの安否情報などを確認できるサービスです）

➡ If you would like to record a message（伝言を録音する場合）
↓
Dial 171（171 をダイヤル）

↓

Press 1（1を入力）

↓

Dial a landline phone number including the area code
（[固定電話] の番号を市外局番から入力）

↓

Then press 1（1を入力）

↓

Record your message of up to 30 seconds in length after the
beep（30秒以内で伝言を録音）

↓

Press 9 to end the message（9を入力して終了）

* To rerecord your message, press 8
　（録音のやり直しは8を入力）

▶ If you would like to check a message（伝言を確認する場合）

↓

Dial 171（171をダイヤル）

↓

Press 2（2を入力）

↓

Dial a landline phone number including the area code
（[固定電話] の番号を市外局番から入力）

↓

Then press 1（1を入力）

↓

The message will begin playing（伝言の再生開始）

↓

* To replay your message, press 8
　（繰り返し再生は8を入力）

* To play the next message, press 9
　（次の伝言再生は9を入力）

* To record your own message after playing a message,
　press 3（再生後の伝言の録音は3を入力）

* There will be a charge for phone usage.
　（通話料金がかかります）

* Contact your service provider for information on how to use this service on anything other than land phones.
（固定電話以外からの利用については各通信事業者にお問い合わせください）

▶ Disaster Emergency Message Board（災害用伝言板）
For details on how to use Disaster Emergency Message Boards, visit your cell phone service provider's website. An explanation of how to use them may be available in English.
（災害用伝言板の使い方は、各キャリアのホームページをご確認ください。英語で利用方法を説明している場合もあります）

NTT(Web171):
https://www.ntt-east.co.jp/saigai/web171/

docomo:
https://www.nttdocomo.co.jp/info/disaster/disaster_board/

SoftBank:
https://www.softbank.jp/mobile/service/dengon/

au:
https://www.au.com/mobile/anti-disaster/saigai-dengon/

* Actual URLs may differ from those listed above.
（上記の URL は変更されることがあります）

災害時に役立つ資料集

警報・注意報

▶特別警報 (Emergency Warnings / Severe Warnings)

2013年8月から運用開始された、「警報の発表基準を上回るような甚大な災害」が起こる可能性がある場合に出されるもの。「数十年に一度レベル」の強度のものに対して適用されます。なお、津波・噴火・地震については、「特別警報」はありません。従来の「大津波警報(Major / Severe Tsunami Warning)」が「特別警報」レベルに相当します。

大雨特別警報 (Heavy Rain Emergency Warning / Severe Heavy Rain Warning)、暴風特別警報 (Storm Emergency Warning / Severe Storm Warning)、暴風雪特別警報 (Storm Emergency Warning / Severe Blizzard Warning)、大雪特別警報 (Storm Emergency Warning / Severe Snowfall Warning)、波浪特別警報 (High Sea Emergency Warning / High Sea Level Warning)、高潮特別警報 (Storm Surge Emergency Warning / Severe Storm Surge Warning) など

▶警報 (Warnings)

重大な災害の起こるおそれがあることを警告するもの。なお、「雷」や「濃霧」などのように、局所的な災害については「警報」は設定されていません。

大雨警報 (Heavy Rain Warning)、洪水警報 (Flood Warning)、暴風警報 (Storm Warning)、暴風雪警報 (Blizzard Warning)、大雪警報 (Heavy Snowfall Warning)、波浪警報 (High Sea Level Warning)、高潮警報 (Storm Surge Warming) など

▶注意報 (Advisories)

災害の起こる恐れがあることを注意するためのもの。Advisory の代わりに Watch を使うこともあります。

大雨注意報 (Heavy Rain Advisory)、洪水注意報 (Flood Advisory)、強風注意報 (Storm Advisory)、風雪注意報 (Blizzard Advisory)、大雪注意報 (Heavy Snowfall Advisory)、波浪注意報 (High Sea Level Advisory)、高潮注意報 (Storm Surge Advisory)、雷注意報 (Lightning Storm Advisory)、融雪注意報 (Snowmelt Advisory)、濃霧注意報 (Dense Fog Advisory) など

アメリカの「MM震度階級」

日本で使われている「震度」は、欧米の人たちにとってはなじみが薄いため、「震度5」などと言われても、直感的に理解できないことが多いようです。アメリカなどでは、一般の人はいわゆる「マグニチュード」による表記になじみがあるようです。以下のような言い方がよく用いられています。

The earthquake was a 5.0 on the Richter Scale.
その地震はマグニチュード 5.0 の強さでした。

このように、「マグニチュード」のことは Richter Scale（リヒタースケール）と呼びます。

日本の震度の感覚がわからないと思われる外国人に地震の震度を説明する場合、例えば、

The earthquake had an intensity of 5 on the Japanese scale of 0 to 7.
その地震は、0 ～ 7 で表す日本の震度階級で言うと、5 の強さでした。

のように言うといいでしょう。なお、アメリカでは「改正メルカリ震度階級（MM震度階、Mercalli intensity scale）」というものが使われており、ⅠからⅫの12段階で強さが表されています。

MM震度階級（アメリカ）と気象庁震度階級（日本）の対応表

MM震度階		気象庁震度
Ⅰ	Instrumental	（きわめて弱い）	0～1
Ⅱ	Feeble	（非常に弱い）	1～2
Ⅲ	Slight	（弱い）	2～3
Ⅳ	Moderate	（中くらい）	3
Ⅴ	Rather Strong	（やや強い）	4
Ⅵ	Strong	（強い）	5弱
Ⅶ	Very Strong	（非常に強い）	5強
Ⅷ	Destructive	（きわめて強い）	6弱
Ⅸ	Ruinous	（破壊的）	6強～7
Ⅹ	Disastrous	（破滅的）	7～
Ⅺ	Very Disastrous	（壊滅的）	7～
Ⅻ	Catastrophic	（絶望的）	7～

噴火警戒レベル

火山の噴火の可能性がある場合、状況の切迫度に応じて、5つの警戒レベルが設定されています。

▶レベル5　避難

実際に噴火が発生したり、あるいは切迫している状況。危険な居住地域からは、避難することが必要になります。

▶レベル4　避難準備

居住地域に重大な被害を及ぼす噴火が起こることが予想される状況。避難の準備を進めることが勧告されます。

▶レベル3　入山規制

居住地域の近くまで被害が及ぶ危険がある噴火が予想される状況。山への登山・入山は規制されます。

▶レベル2　火口周辺規制

火口周辺に影響を及ぼす噴火が発生した場合、あるいは発生が予想される状況。火口付近への立ち入りは規制されます。

▶レベル1　平常

平常通りの火山活動が見られる状況。状況に応じて、火口内への立ち入りは規制されます。

火山ガスレベルに関する注意報・警報

火山ガスの注意報・警報は、二酸化硫黄（SO_2 / Sulfur Dioxide）の濃度により、4つのレベルが設定されています。

レベル4：一般警報　　　　　　5.0 ppm 以上
レベル3：一般注意報　　　　　2.0 ppm ～ 5.0 ppm
レベル2：高感受性者警報 *　　0.6 ppm ～ 2.0 ppm
レベル1：高感受性者注意報 *　0.2 ppm ～ 0.6 ppm

*「高感受性者注意報・警報」は、一般の人には問題のないレベルだとされています。

□被災	
遺体	body, remains
一部損壊	partially destroyed
運休	out of service
瓦礫	rubble, debris
義援金	donation
帰宅困難者	commuters unable to return home
帰宅支援マップ	emergency map for getting home, in-case-of-emergency commuter map
給水車	water tank truck
計画停電	scheduled power outage
激甚災害地	disaster zone
（飛行機の）欠航	cancellation of flight
公衆電話	pay phone, public phone
災害	disaster
災害時帰宅支援ステーション	support spot for disaster victims unable to go home
災害用伝言ダイヤル	disaster message dial
死者	the dead
死傷者	dead and injured, casualties
地震酔い	phantom quake (syndrome)
震災ストレス	post-quake trauma
心的外傷後ストレス障害	post-traumatic stress disorder, PTSD
心理カウンセラー	psychologist
ストレス反応	stress response
精神科医	psychiatrist
生存罪悪感	survivor's guilt
生存者	survivor
生存者症候群	survivor syndrome
全壊	completely destroyed

災害時に役立つ資料集

大災害	catastrophe, major disaster
炊き出し	emergency food service, preparing meals outdoors
断水	water outage, water failure
停電	blackout, power failure, power outage
撤去する	remove, take away
倒壊	collapse
半壊	half destroyed
被害（額）	damage
被災者	disaster victim
被災地	disaster area
避難者	evacuee
負傷者	the injured, the wounded
フラッシュバック	flashback
振替輸送	transferring passengers onto other trains
行方不明者	the missing
ライフライン	essential utilities
臨床心理士	clinical psychologist

□人命救助

医療品	medical supplies
浮き輪	lifesaver
応急手当	first aid
海上保安庁	Coast Guard
監視員	watchman
救急車	ambulance
救助犬	rescue dog
救助活動	rescue work
救助船	rescue ship
救助隊、救急隊	rescue team
救助ヘリ	rescue helicopter
救命胴衣	life-jacket, life vest
救命ボート	rescue boat
緊急対策本部	disaster[emergency] headquarters
災害救助法	Disaster Relief Act
三角巾	sling
自衛隊	Japan Self-Defense Force
重機	heavy machinery
消毒液	antiseptic
消防車	fire engine

食料不足	food supply shortages
担架	stretcher
トリアージ（重症度判定検査）	triage
ペースメーカー	pacemaker
ライフセーバー	lifeguard

避難

一時避難場所	temporary evacuation site
緩降機	emergency rappel rope, descending lifeline
救助袋	⇒脱出用シュート
広域避難場所	regional evacuation site
自主避難	voluntary evacuation
脱出用シュート	emergency evacuation chute
津波避難指定ビル	designated tsunami evacuation building
津波避難タワー	tsunami evacuation tower
非常階段	fire escape, escape stair(case)
非常口	emergency exit
非常灯	emergency light
非常用すべり台	evacuation slide
非常用持ち出し袋	emergency pack, survival kit
避難	evacuation
避難勧告	evacuation advisory
避難口誘導灯	emergency light, guide light
避難訓練	emergency drill, evacuation drill
避難指示	evacuation instruction
避難所	shelter
避難ばしご	escape ladder

非常用持ち出し袋の中身・非常用備蓄品

アルファ米	cooked and dried rice
印鑑	personal seal[stamp]
インスタントラーメン	instant noodles
飲料水	drinking water
懐中電灯	flash light
カセットコンロ	portable gas stove[burner]
カップ麺	cup noodles
紙コップ	paper cup
紙皿	paper plate
ガムテープ	packing tape

乾パン	dried bread, hardtack
救急箱	first-aid kit
給水用ポリタンク	plastic water container
軍手	cotton work gloves
携帯電話充電器	mobile telephone charger
携帯ラジオ	portable radio
工具セット	tool kit
ゴム手袋	rubber gloves
ちり取り	dustpan
通帳	account book
使い捨てカイロ	disposable heating pad
ティッシュペーパー	tissue, Kleenex
投光器	floodlight
長靴	boots
バケツ	bucket
発電機	generator
絆創膏	bandage, Band-Aid
非常食	emergency food, provisions
ビニール袋	plastic bag
ブルーシート	blue plastic sheet
ヘルメット	helmet, hard hat
ほうき	broom
防塵マスク	(dust) mask
水のいらないシャンプー	dry shampoo
無線機	radio
メガホン	megaphone
ラップフィルム	plastic wrap
ランタン	lantern
レトルト食品	retort food
割りばし	disposable chopsticks

□地震	
液状化現象	ground liquefaction
S 波	S-wave, secondary[shear] wave
活断層	active fault
巨大地震	huge earthquake, enormous earthquake, megaquake
緊急地震速報	earthquake early warning, EEW
震源地	epicenter
震度	intensity

たて揺れ	vertical oscillation
小さな地震	tremor
直下型地震	inland earthquake
南海トラフ	Nankai Trough
P波	P-wave, primary[pressure] wave
本震	main shock
マグニチュード	magnitude
無感地震	unfelt earthquake
有感地震	felt earthquake
よこ揺れ	horizontal oscillation
余震	aftershock

□津波

大津波警報	severe tsunami warning
津波	tsunami, tidal wave
津波危険区域	tsunami hazard zone
津波警報	tsunami warning
津波注意報	tsunami advisory
津波到達時刻	tsunami arrival time
津波の高さ	tsunami height
堤防	levee

□火災

火災旋風	firestorm
火災報知器	smoke detector, fire alarm
消火器	fire extinguisher
消火訓練	firefighting training
消火栓	fire hydrant
初期消火班	initial fire extinguishing squad
スプリンクラー	fire sprinkler
バケツリレー	bucket brigade
防火シャッター	fire shutter
防火扉	fire door, FDR
ホース	hose

□風水害・雷雨

稲妻	lightning
雷警報	lightning warning
局地的大雨	local heavy rain

決壊	washout
ゲリラ豪雨	sudden heavy rain
洪水	flood
集中豪雨	⇒局地的大雨
浸水	flood
水没する、冠水する	swamp, submerge
台風	typhoon
高潮警報	storm surge warning
竜巻	tornado, twister
竜巻注意情報	tornado alert, tornado warning
ダムの決壊	dam collapse
超大型台風	super typhoon
低気圧	low pressure
都市型水害	urban flood
突風	gust of wind
土嚢	flood bags
爆弾低気圧	bomb low pressure
風速	wind speed
暴風域	storm area, violent wind zone
床上浸水	above-floor-level flooding
雷雨	thunderstorm
雷雲	thunder cloud
雷鳴	thunder
離岸流	rip current

□雪害	
除雪する	clear the snow off
除雪道具	snow shoveling gear
スタッドレスタイヤ	⇒冬用タイヤ
タイヤチェーン	snow chain
雪崩	(snow) avalanche
冬用タイヤ	winter tire
猛吹雪	blizzard, violent snowstorm

□土砂災害	
崖崩れ	landslide
山体崩壊	sector collapse
地すべり	landslide
斜面崩壊	slope failure

鉄砲水	flash flood
土砂崩れ	mudslide
土砂災害危険箇所	landslide-prone spot
土砂災害危険区域	landslide-prone area
土砂災害警戒情報	landslide warning notice
土石流	mudslide
落石	falling rock

□原発事故

原子力発電所	atomic power plant
NBC 防護服	nuclear-biological-chemical suit
水蒸気爆発	steam explosion
水素爆発	hydrogen explosion
電源喪失	loss of power
非常電源	emergency power supply
被ばく	exposure
ベント、放出	ventilation
放射性物質	radioactive material
放射線検査	radiation inspection
放射線防護服	radiation protection suit
放射線量	radiation dose
放射能測定器	radiation detector
ホットスポット	hot spot
メルトスルー	meltthrough
メルトダウン	meltdown
臨界事故	criticality accident

□噴火

火口	crater
火砕流	pyroclastic flow
火山	volcano
火山ガス	volcanic gas
火山弾	volcanic bomb
火山泥流	volcanic mud flow
火山灰	volcanic ash
活火山	active volcano
噴火	eruption
噴火警報	volcanic eruption warning
溶岩流	lava flow

□その他の災害・事故・事件	
隕石落下	meteorite fall
強盗	burglary
自爆テロ	suicide attack, suicide bombing
集団感染	group infection
食中毒	food poisoning
地割れ	cracks in the ground
脱水症状	dehydration
熱中症	heat stroke
爆弾テロ	terrorist bombing
ひき逃げ	hit-and-run
雹	hail
暴動	riot
漏電	short circuit

□防災	
安全管理者	⇒防災担当者
火災保険	fire insurance
救急救命室	emergency room, ER
救急救命センター	medical emergency center
事業継続計画	business continuity planning, BCP
地震保険	earthquake insurance
耐火性	fire resistance
耐震基準	antiseismic standards
耐震構造	aseismatic structure
耐震診断	seismic resistance evaluation
耐震補強	antiseismic reinforcement
非常用電源	emergency power
非常用呼び出しボタン	emergency call button
避雷針	lightning rod
防火水槽	fire-prevention water tank
防災	disaster prevention
防災訓練	emergency drill
防災公園	disaster prevention park
防災センター	disaster prevention center
防災対策	disaster prevention measures
防災担当者	safety officer
防災用品	emergency supplies
防災林	disaster-prevention forest

免震構造	quake-absorbing structure
夜警	night watch

□防災・防犯・事故防止グッズ

ガラス飛散防止フィルム	shatterproof film
固定器具	anti-toppling device
自転車かご用カバー［ネット］	bicycle's basket cover[net]
人感センサー付き照明器具	light equipped with motion-sensors
つっぱり棒	tension rod
転倒防止器具	⇒固定器具
踏み抜き防止用長靴	puncture resistant boots
防炎物品	fireproof product
防火布	fireproof cloth
防災頭巾	fireproof hood, disaster hood
防犯ブザー	(personal) alarm
補助錠	auxiliary lock

□証明書類等

DNA鑑定	DNA test
健康保険証	health insurance card[certificate]
国民保健	national health insurance
在留カード	residence card
車検証	vehicle inspection certificate
住民票	certificate of residence
特別永住者証明書	special permanent resident certificate
歯型	tooth mark

□場所・施設・設備

空き地	open area
エスカレーター	escalator
エレベーター	elevator
仮設住宅	temporary housing
交通機関	transit, transportation
校庭	schoolyard
コンセント	(electrical) outlet
昇降口	entrance
地下街	underground mall
駐車場	parking lot
超高層ビル	high-rise building, skyscraper

災害時に役立つ資料集

プレーカー	fuse box, circuit breaker
木造住宅	wooden house, wooden building

□避難所生活	
エコノミークラス症候群	economy class syndrome
仮設トイレ	temporary bathroom
紙おむつ	(disposable) diaper
簡易トイレ	portable toilet
救援物資	⇒支援物資
共同浴場	public bathing
血圧計	blood pressure meter
粉ミルク缶	powdered baby formula can
シーツ	sheet
支援物資	relief supplies
授乳用ケープ	nursing cover
生理用品	sanitary products
洗濯物	laundry
洗面設備	washing facilities
伝言板	bulletin board, message board
布団	futon, bed, bed comforter
哺乳瓶	baby bottle
枕	pillow
毛布	blanket
燃えないゴミ	unburnable garbage
燃えるゴミ	burnable garbage

世界の緊急通報用電話番号

■北アメリカ

	警察	救急	消防
アメリカ	911	911	911
カナダ	911	911	911
メキシコ	060	060	060

■オセアニア

	警察	救急	消防
オーストラリア	000	000	000
ニュージーランド	111	111	111

■アジア

	警察	救急	消防
タイ	191	1669	199
ベトナム	113	115	114
中国	110	120	119
韓国	112	119	119
シンガポール	999	995	995
インド	100	102	101

■ヨーロッパ

	警察	救急	消防
フランス	17	15	18
ドイツ	110	112	112
イギリス	999	999	999
スペイン	112	112	112
イタリア	113	118	118
ロシア	02	03	01

■中近東・アフリカ

	警察	救急	消防
エジプト	122	123	180
南アフリカ	10111	10177	10111

災害時に役立つ資料集

非常用持出品チェックシート

Keep these items in an emergency pack and keep them handy
非常用持ち出し袋にこれらの物品を入れ、すぐに持ち出せる場所に
置いておきましょう。

▶ Valuables　貴重品類

- ☐ cash (including some 10-yen coins for making phone calls)
  現金（電話をかけるための10円玉も含む）
- ☐ bank book　預金通帳
- ☐ seal　印鑑
- ☐ health insurance ID card　保険証
- ☐ driver's license　運転免許証

▶ Evacuation goods　避難用具

- ☐ flashlight　懐中電灯
- ☐ dry-cell batteries　乾電池
- ☐ portable radio　携帯ラジオ
- ☐ helmet　ヘルメット
- ☐ disaster hood　防災頭巾
- ☐ flare　発煙筒
- ☐ whistle　笛
- ☐ portable eating utensils　携帯調理器具

▶ General items　生活用品

- ☐ blanket　毛布
- ☐ can opener　缶切り
- ☐ matches / lighter　マッチ・ライター
- ☐ knife　ナイフ
- ☐ portable toilet　携帯用トイレ
- ☐ first-aid kit　救急用具
- ☐ medicine / medication　常用薬
- ☐ sanitary products　生理用品

▶ Emergency food　非常食

- ☐ hardtack　乾パン
- ☐ canned foods　缶詰
- ☐ sweets and snacks　甘いお菓子やスナック
- ☐ bottled water　ペットボトル入り飲料水
- ☐ instant noodles　インスタントラーメン

▶ Clothing　衣料品

- ☐ gloves　手袋
- ☐ undergarments　下着
- ☐ socks　靴下
- ☐ long-sleeved shirts　長そでシャツ
- ☐ pants　長ズボン
- ☐ sweaters　セーター
- ☐ rain gear　雨具

緊急時の連絡先メモ

名前 Name

(保護者の名前) Parent's or Guardian's Name

住所 Address

自宅の電話番号 Phone Number

携帯電話番号 Cellphone Number

学校・勤務先 Name of School / Worksite

電話番号 Phone Number

血液型 Blood Type

持病 Chronic Diseases

Memo

....

....

....

....

....

....

....

....

....

....

Memo

Memo

【著者紹介】

デイビッド・A・セイン David A. Thayne

米国生まれ。豊富な英語の教授経験を生かし、数多くの英語関係書籍を執筆している。著書に『製造現場の英語』『ビジネス英語手帳 使えるフレーズ1800』（アスク出版）、『爆笑！英語コミックエッセイ 日本人のちょっとヘンな英語』（アスコム）など多数。

現在、英語を中心テーマとしてさまざまな企画を実現する AtoZ を主宰。東京根津および春日にて英語学校も経営している。

Webサイト：https://www.smartenglish.co.jp

【執筆協力】

森田 修、小林 奈々子、Jamie Jose、Malcolm Hendricks、Nancy Velasquez、Sean McGee

〈増補改訂版〉災害時の英語

2014年5月25日	初版	第1刷
2020年9月26日	第2版	第1刷

著者	デイビッド・A・セイン
発行者	天谷 修身
発行	株式会社アスク出版
	〒162-8558　東京都新宿区下宮比町2-6
	電話：03-3267-6864
	FAX：03-3267-6867
	https://www.ask-books.com/

装幀	岡崎 裕樹（アスク出版）
本文デザイン・DTP	一柳 茂（クリエーターズユニオン）
音声収録・編集	アスク出版 映像事業部
印刷・製本	株式会社光邦
編集担当	竹田 直次（アスク出版）

ISBN978-4-86639-358-2　　　　　　Printed in Japan